It's Not Where You Start...

Jan Swallow

Michael Terence Publishing

This edition first published in paperback by
Michael Terence Publishing in 2021
www.mtp.agency

ISBN 9781800942394

Cover image
by Anna Sims

Cover design

Jan Swallow

Contents

Foreword

"It's Not Where You Start" is not so much a family saga but rather my "Tales of the Unexpected".

I recall events unique to my life. On qualifying as a doctor I did not set out to pursue any set ambition but rather determined to enjoy my chosen career in full, wherever it might take me. A choice I do not regret as now I share some of my experiences with my readers.

My Arrival and What Followed…

I was born on the sixth of September 1934.

Life is never straight forward, and from day one, mine was true to form. For the home delivery of my brother Hugh in 1931, my mother had the assistance of a midwife who had been recommended by our old Scots doctor, Dr Robertson. It was a difficult birth, and the midwife was good, so three years later she was booked again. In the meantime, she had become well known and very busy. When Mummy's time came this midwife had been off work for some time with a septic thumb. Remember, these are the days pre-NHS and pre antibiotics. She came back to deliver me before her infection was cleared. Although the delivery of a 5½lb infant was normal, nothing else was so. Her sepsis resulted in infection all round the family. Most importantly, Mummy, on the third day after my birth was rushed to the Isolation Hospital with puerperal sepsis, a truly life-threatening infection. My brother developed such a severe ear infection that the doctor was debating whether he should go to Great Ormond Street Children's Hospital, London, with mastoiditis, and my grandmother, caring for the family, developed quinsy, a severe throat infection, again in those days, a life-threatening illness.

What about me? Three days old, no breastfeeding, no cuddling with mother or father I was quickly sent off to neighbours to be looked after.

In the garden with Mummy and Brother, Hugh

They rushed to the local chemist for a glass feeding bottle, teats and Cow & Gate and I survived, not having the infection that affected the others. Meanwhile, doubts were expressed at the hospital whether Mummy would survive. She hallucinated for many days and did not know anyone. It was agreed that I should be called Marjorie, in her memory, and the paternal grandparents arrived from Marlow, Bucks, to take over caring for the family. My maternal grandmother went home to fight her infection away from the family.

Mummy did survive and returned home after a month in isolation. I remember her telling me she had quinine injections every few hours, and they were painful. For several days, her temperature was 104°C and it seemed impossible to bring it down, despite tepid sponging regularly.

Once home, gradually things returned to a more normal atmosphere. Hugh recovered, but was always susceptible to ear infection. Grandmother, Nanny, also survived quinsy, and became a family carer as Mummy slowly recovered and was able to leave the bedroom.

As for me? I don't know, nobody has ever mentioned how I coped, but one thing I do know. That time meant I never bonded with my mother. This took me a long time to connect to the fact that our relationship was always a difficult one.

Years later Mummy told me that when Dr Robertson visited her at home, she told him that the midwife had not submitted her bill. For the only time in the many years he was our GP, Dr Robertson swore! "I should think not" with an expletive. "She knows what she's done!" At which point he threw his homburg hat across the bedroom in anger.

Meanwhile Mummy, having lost her very pretty curly hair after her treatment gradually regained her strength. By which time I was three months old and surviving despite it all.

One collects anecdotes of early years. It is easy to imagine memories of being a toddler, but really, it is simply a way of holding on to what appeals to you, coming from conversation within the family and vague mind's eye images of one's own.

I have my own little pictures of me at three. Mummy told me that I could sing in tune by the time I was two whilst in my pram. The song? A nice cup of tea! Now sung by my grandchildren, but not aged three.

But one memory is my very own, and oh so hazy. A family holiday in Bournemouth in 1938. I simply remember a ring of bright orange melon in a sea of green jelly. No sand, no sea, no donkey rides, no bucket and spade. Just being inseparable from my teddy, Rupert, and green jelly!

I was 5 on September 6th, 1939. I was aware that something was up as we sat around our Pye wireless with its sunray front.

I watched my parents faces at the end of August when we heard that we were at war with Germany. I didn't know what was meant but it seemed to involve everybody in activity.

A woman's work is never done

With Rupert aged 3

The wireless kept us informed and we were exhorted to find something we could do for the war effort. Dig for victory became a slogan to follow as playing fields were ploughed up and potatoes planted. Iron railings disappeared to make munitions and black out curtains were made. Soon we heard the cry put that light out from the Air Raid Wardens. My fifth birthday is still memorable to me over 80 years later. Why? Not for the party or the birthday tea. No, in the strange world in which my brother and I found ourselves everything was changing. There is no other birthday I can remember when I could tell you what presents I received. But 1939 was very different.

A few days earlier we had taken in 2 boys, about 7 and 9, evacuees from London as bombing of the city was anticipated. My father was not about as Mummy welcomed these two with their small suitcase and cardboard gas mask cases. It was all very strange for a little 5 year old getting excited, not about a war, but a birthday. Why was Daddy not around? As a schoolmaster he had the task of being billeting officer for the homes in Luton, Bedfordshire. For three days he met trains from London and took parties of evacuees round the town calling door to door asking for householders to offer them accommodation. Meanwhile Mummy was doing her bit for the war effort by taking the 2 boys into our 3-bed semidetached house.

So, on the day of my birthday, I was not greeted with Happy Birthday to you being sung, but the sound of the first air raid siren. A degree of panic must have followed. I think Mummy remembering the first world war, thought that the raid would involve gas. Instructions had been given by wireless and posters about what to do. Into the large stone kitchen sink went heavy blankets to soak. These would cover us if gas warnings came. None did. We had had no time to build air raid shelters, so two evacuees and my brother and I were deposited under the heaviest thing in the house, the kitchen table. This is a vivid memory, for here we stayed with the memorable birthday presents – a panda nightdress case, and a zoo – with metal cages to make up to enclose the elephant, tiger, lion, polar bear and giraffe which the colourful box contained. Soon the all clear sounded and we discovered that this had been a practice alert. It was followed over the next four years by a good many more alerts which were the real thing. Why Luton was thought a wise place to move children from London 30 miles south east of us still puzzles me. Whilst it was famous as the centre of the straw hat industry at that time, it still had many sites which were of importance to the war effort, and thus a target for German bombs. And so later they proved to be. Vauxhall motors, Electrolux, Skefko ball bearings, Commer cars, were all heavily involved in making vital parts for vehicles, weapons and other equipment needed for troops mobilised from among men in the town. These were soon to leave behind a town where women took on the roles of their menfolk before the war.

Our two evacuees seemed very strange to me and were, I would say, worldly wise and streetwise, compared with Hugh and me. My father, a strict disciplinarian, left Mummy to admonish them, if needed. And it certainly was needed, I now know, for they took great delight in showing Hugh and I what fun it was to deliberately urinate in their bed. So curious for us to watch.

They had an elder sister who was billeted not far away. She began calling in, offering to run errands for Mummy. This was gratefully accepted until it was discovered that she pocketed the money and stole the goods.

I don't remember how long they stayed with us, but soon it seemed they all three headed back to the East End. This was the time of the phoney war when in that autumn of 1939 not a lot happened. From my little world view, it was all fun, because the autumn days were sunny, schools were closed in September and early October, and there was time to play. My brother and I did our bit for the war effort by buying six day-old chicks from the market. We brought them home in a Weetabix box and made a house for them in a box lined with newspapers and grass. They didn't survive long, and we would come down in the morning to find a little stiff yellow fluffy ball in the box.

However, two did begin to thrive and became less attractive as they changed colour to brown and grew feathers. It soon became clear that the larger of the two was pecking the other one all the time. It was not helping our egg production enterprise being the dominant male. He was soon the last of the six.

At this time, I had a hessian gardening apron which I loved because it had a large pocket in which to store many treasures. Fun for me, was to pedal my tricycle up and down the road with my horrid chicken in the apron pocket. I would accost any neighbour I passed with, "Have you seen Hitler?" followed by a dramatic opening of the apron pocket with, "He's here." Soon I was being asked by neighbours how Hitler was and was quite pleased when eventually I could reply – "He's dead."

Another vivid memory comes to mind. All four of us had taken the bus into the country north of Luton to the village of Barton at the north eastern end of the Chiltern Hills. Here we picnicked at Barton Springs, playing in the water and beside it as the air raid warning sounded. Daddy organised us to climb up high into the hills, so we looked down onto the deep valley which held the Springs. As we sat on the hillside, a monoplane flew below us up the valley. We could see the pilot putting on his leather helmet as he flew past and we looked down into his cockpit. What did this mean? Sadly, it meant that all the planes at Luton's airport, then very small, had been scrambled anticipating a bomb on the airfield. The bomb sadly was a land mine, which dropped near Vauxhall Motors, close to the airport, with considerable loss of civilian life. We really were at war.

1940

School In War Time

My memory of infants school, Old Bedford Road, Luton focuses mainly on war experiences. We walked everywhere. Cars were a luxury we could not afford. Mummy walked with me to and from school. Daddy and brother Hugh, 3 years older than me, were at Hitchin Road Junior School where Daddy was headmaster.

I loved learning. My first teacher, Miss Orchard called out my name Janice. I did not respond. Frustrated teacher. When I got home, I asked Mummy, "What is my name?" "Of course, you know your name." "No Mummy, what is my real name?" I had always been Jan and so ignored the teacher at school.

My next class teacher, Miss Spooner, made a pet of me, I now know, although I was unaware at the time. I learned quickly and she was also surprised at how well I could knit at just six. Because I finished my sums ahead of time, she set me making a pair of knitted gloves for my mother for Christmas. A simple pattern in plain stitch and on two needles. The headmistress Miss Chamberlain found me knitting at the back of the class and I think admonished my class teacher for the indulgence. I also recollect going with Mummy to tea with Miss Spooner.

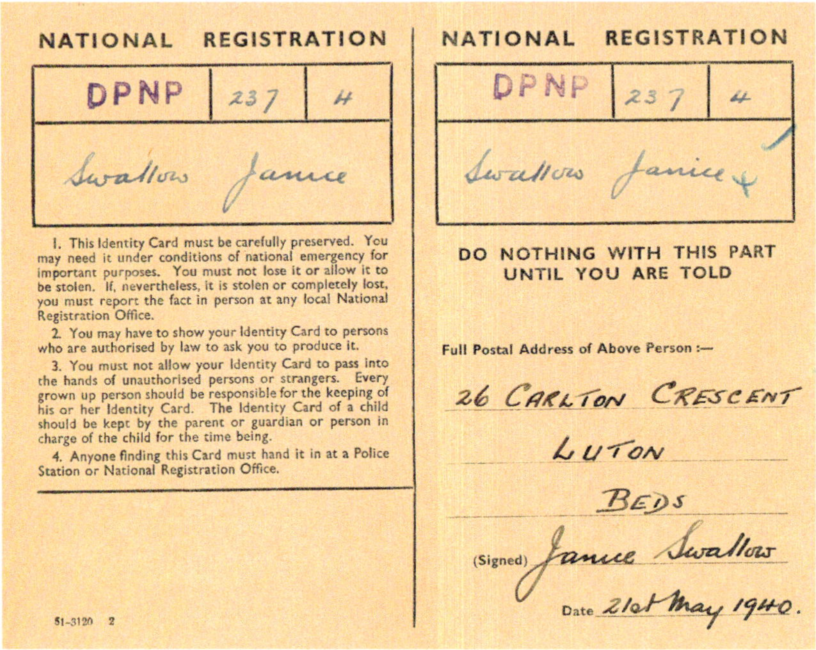

NATIONAL REGISTRATION

DPNP | 237 | 4

Swallow Janice

1. This Identity Card must be carefully preserved. You may need it under conditions of national emergency for important purposes. You must not lose it or allow it to be stolen. If, nevertheless, it is stolen or completely lost, you must report the fact in person at any local National Registration Office.

2. You may have to show your Identity Card to persons who are authorised by law to ask you to produce it.

3. You must not allow your Identity Card to pass into the hands of unauthorised persons or strangers. Every grown up person should be responsible for the keeping of his or her Identity Card. The Identity Card of a child should be kept by the parent or guardian or person in charge of the child for the time being.

4. Anyone finding this Card must hand it in at a Police Station or National Registration Office.

51-3120 2

NATIONAL REGISTRATION

DPNP | 237 | 4

Swallow Janice

DO NOTHING WITH THIS PART UNTIL YOU ARE TOLD

Full Postal Address of Above Person :—

26 CARLTON CRESCENT

LUTON

BEDS

(Signed) Janice Swallow

Date 21st May 1940.

We are at war

My Nanny, Mummy's mother taught me to knit aged 5 and Mummy taught me to sew at the same age. Hemming, a little bit of this and a little bit of that which I say to this day when hemming anything and, for knitting, up, over, through, off.

The most significant day in my infants school was a long one and on reflection, frightening, although I wasn't frightened at the time. Having arrived in school at about 8.45, we were settling into class when the air raid warning sounded. We were shepherded into the primitive air raid shelter, dug below the playground. Earth walls, hurricane lamps, and a wooden bench along the walls. We sat, feeling damp and apprehensive for some time until we heard and felt a loud explosion, followed by debris falling down the steps into the shelter. Some children cried. I remained silent and I remember feeling quite composed! After 2-3 hours the lamps went out which added to the anxiety. The teachers, who must have been very stressed, tried to keep us amused and calm. So many songs were sung, One man went to mow, Ten green bottles (which I have been unwilling to sing ever since), numerous nursery rhymes and counting games.

Meanwhile, as we approached end of morning school, and after the All Clear had sounded Mummy arrived at Old Bedford Road on her way to take me home to lunch, only to be stopped by a barrier and policeman about 150 yards from the school. She was told there had been a hit on the school and the road was closed. Mummy, who was not a composed individual collapsed and was taken into a nearby house for hot sweet tea. It must have been agonising for her to wait patiently until she was allowed through with the other mums about 3 hours later.

What had happened that morning was that a German bomber had dropped a large bomb which landed, not on the school, but on the hat factory opposite. Luton until the mid-60s was noted for hat manufacture of all kinds. The rubble clearance, to release us little ones from the shelter, took until mid-afternoon. We climbed out to find white faced parents waiting at the school gate. I remember vividly thinking how pretty the fallen telegraph wires looked because they were strewn with the various coloured ribbons which were used in trimming the hats. I was not aware that many girls and older women lost their lives at their workplace that day.

Another memory is of walking home hand in hand with Mummy and saying to her -"they told us two buses had crashed, but I knew what had happened."

From day one I loved learning, anything. Being at infants school at the beginning of the war however brought disadvantages. I hated gas mask practice, which seemed to occur frequently. I remember hiding under my desk rather than put on this black mask, which steamed up inside as one breathed. It was the smell I hated until a little school friend – Leonard Brightman, who wore corduroy shorts with pearl buttons up the side, said, "Do what my mummy does. She puts scent in mine." Problem solved, Evening in Paris or Californian Poppy, both from Woolworths did the trick. Nights spent in air raid shelters did not help concentration at school, but I lapped up learning – reading especially. Daddy was a great influence and encouragement.

Being a head teacher himself he guided my learning. I have happy memories of sitting on the arm of his chair whilst he read poetry to me from Palgrave's Golden Treasury. "Here's one you'll like" he would say as he chose a poem, and of course I did. My love of poetry and rhyme must have started then age 7, thanks to his influence. I was soon writing poems of my own and had a special book to write them in, very carefully. I have it still.

Daddy digging for victory

From my infants' school I moved on to Hitchin Road Junior School where my father was headmaster. A mixed blessing being a pupil in your father's school. Always conspicuous, although not wishing to be, and a target for jealousy, although I cannot say I was a victim of this and had many friends. The school was in a deprived area of the town and it was many years later, on reflection when I realised how poor many of the pupils were. Daddy was a father figure to so many of the mothers, many of whom had husbands in the forces and were coping alone in hardship. I sat next to Doris Wright. I admired her enormously for her way of coping with a runny nose – which she had most of the time. Doris had knickers where the elastic had gone from one leg, so it always hung at half mast, below her knee and showing below her dirty cotton dress. I watched closely as the yellow mucous emerged from her nostril and ran down towards her mouth, only to be sniffed up loudly at the brink and disappearing up her nostril again. I was fascinated and longed to be able to copy her. Eventually when I had a cold the technique was perfected and a down-up was achieved. The only snag was that perfection came at the dinner table at home producing a roar of disgust from father and brother. I was admonished never to do it again, despite my plea, "But Doris Wright always does it." Poor Doris. She always had a filthy hanky pinned to her dress, but never used it.

School medical inspections were scary times. I always worried that the doctor would find something wrong with me, although I don't remember ever being ill, apart from childhood infections. I suppose I knew I was always the smallest in the class but could hold my own with the big boys. A fun memory was of the medical I had when about 8. These took place in Daddy's study, where there was a welcome coal fire. The lady doctor said, "Well you're fine but when are you going to grow?" To which I replied, "I know, but I can stand on my head and sing God Save the King. Foolishly she said, "Let's see you do that." I up ended myself and sang the national anthem, not once, but on and on until persuaded to come down. I reckon there were a few smiles behind my back. My talent to stand on my head stayed with me. The final time was at the age of 56 in far more auspicious circumstances, - but more of that many moons later in this saga.

There was little crime of which I as a child was aware in this time of war. Doors were left unlocked, bicycles were propped, unpadlocked against the wall. I hated school dinners – horrible gristly meat in greasy stews. Having tried them I opted to walk home to lunch and back in the afternoon. I marvel at this now, for my route took me across roads and public parks. A distance of 1½ miles at least which I did four times a day on my own unless Daddy took me to school on the crossbar of his bike. Sometimes I was aware of odd men in the park looking at me, or couples making love among the bushes, but I had a canny sixth sense when to take to my heels and run, and never came to any harm. In the same park about 5-6 years later I was playing tennis when I was aware of a young man exposing himself on the surrounding grass outside the court. I think confidence came to me because the netting round the tennis courts was between us, but I walked up to him and told him that I would get the park keeper at once unless he put that thing away. He fled. Tackling problems came to me early in life.

About this time, I began to learn to play the violin. Music was important at home. Mummy and Daddy both had good voices and sang in the choir at the congregational chapel where they were members and where my brother and I attended Sunday School for many years. Brother Hugh and Daddy played the piano. Mummy played by ear and was an asset for children's parties when she could play for musical party games. It was assumed that we would enjoy standing round the piano singing hymns on Sunday evenings. I can only remember how tired I felt and how I was longing to go to bed.

My music lessons weekly were with Professor Dawson. I found him deadly dull and uninspiring. I practised in fits and starts, but on reflection must have made progress for I was taken round to church halls etc to perform to women's afternoon social groups. It was not until I was at the High School that I found more fun playing in school orchestras. I loved music and was content to listen to all music on the wireless. It is surprising now to think how little opportunity there was in war time Luton to hear professional players of any sort. At junior school, my father introduced everyone in morning assembly to classical music via the wind-up gramophone. I still can visualise his descriptions of the Sorcerer's Apprentice and Beethoven's Pastoral Symphony. He painted pictures in words for us in preparation for what we were to hear. He was ahead of his time in education in many ways. He wrote junior science books which were in print and bringing royalties to my mother long after he had died at the age of 66.

Not only did I dislike the school dinners but also the third of a pint of milk available at morning playtime. The milk monitor, a very senior position, brought in the metal crates early in the school day and left them on the classroom floor. Unfortunately, they were left over the grating above the heating pipes. When time came to pop the paper straw through the cardboard top to the bottle, the milk was slightly warm and smelled horrid. Not for me.

Meanwhile the war in Europe continued and after a lull in air raids we were again spending nights in the air raid shelter. When London was at the height of the bombing my father took us out of the shelter one night to see the red glow in the sky. He told us that bombs had fallen from our town all the way to London and that is what we saw. In the last year of the war the V1 doodlebug bombs began to target Southern England. Being unmanned missiles, it was impossible to work out where they might land. The unmistakable drone of a V1, rather like a car with a dodgy battery, was distinctive and we knew that when it cut out, we had but a short time to take cover. The most memorable attack came however from a V2, a rocket. These were much more powerful and destructive than the V1s. I think now, over 75 years later, it is still the loudest sound I have ever heard. The V2 fell some miles away across the town but as we sat at our desk in our Victorian classroom the impact of the shockwave blew us from our chairs and the dust of ages fell from the rafters. Very frightening. It was only when I returned home that I heard what damage had been done by this evil missile. It had landed on the industrial area in the town which housed Commer Cars and Electrolux and Skefko Ball Bearing factories. Loss of life was considerable. All in the waiting room of a doctor's surgery were killed, as was the doctor himself.

We had no telephone and so it was with great

consternation that my father had to continue at school not knowing if our home, and mummy, were safe. We lived about a mile from the site of the rocket. On coming home, I saw that glass from blown out windows was all around. Fortunately for our house, Mummy had opened all the windows that morning, it being a lovely spring day, giving the house an airing. So, our windows were saved.

1945

Peace At Last and a New School

The end of the war coincided with the end of my schooling with my father. I went to Luton High School for Girls in September 1945 at just 11, having passed the first 11 plus exam which came with free admission to what had been a fee-paying school. The high school was a hundred yards up the road from home, which was wonderful for me after my days of four walks to and from school from 7 years old. I loved it. School uniform, big girls to admire, airy classrooms and real playing fields and playgrounds. Even a swimming pool and gym. I was in my element, but I had a nasty experience within a few weeks of arriving.

With the ending of fee-paying education, it was fortunately possible for all pupils to be admitted following the intelligence tests of 11-plus. So, two other girls came from Hitchin Road School. I was unaware of them and their home circumstances at the time but now I know that they were out of their comfort zone. I suppose they found it difficult to fit in. These were not times when counselling and support for pupils was reckoned necessary. The first I was aware of anything untoward was when I was summoned to see the headmistress, Miss Helen Sheldon. I must give a word picture of this maiden lady for readers to understand how frightening it was for me, the smallest girl in the school, to stand before her in her study. She had come from Cheltenham Ladies College to make ladies out of the mixed bunch of girls at Luton High School. She was large and stately, wearing buttoned shoes, thick grey stockings and shapeless long dresses. Her grey hair was in two plaits across the crown of her head. She crept round the school spying in through corridor windows on the lessons. Her staff were in awe of her, probably frightened of her. So to be sent to see her was scary. I stood in front of her desk as she told me that I had been very unkind to talk about the two girls from my junior school to other girls in the first form, telling them how poor these two were. I was dumb and confused. I had spoken to no-one. Indeed, I had seen very little of these two who were not in my class. "I'm sure your father would not like to hear that you had been telling tales Janice." "No Miss Sheldon." I was terrified. I didn't know what she was talking about, but obviously the two girls had constructed the story about me, possibly being jealous of me. Soon after this they left the school. But untiI I was in my twenties I was so shocked by the accusation that I spoke to no-one about it. I suppose I was also afraid that Miss Sheldon had told my father whom she knew very well. How interesting it is that one can be made to feel ashamed even when one knows that one has done nothing wrong.

My first year was joyous after this. I loved the lessons, I loved the games, I had many friends and was delighted when my class voted for me to be form captain. This meant a special band on my arm and responsibility. Something that started then and stayed with me. On reflection much of what I am was moulded in those days at the High School.

Throughout my time at the High School, I found much to enjoy. I found that I had some skills at sports and played netball, hockey, tennis and rounders with great enthusiasm, and, I say immodestly, some success. Although I was well below average height – what one aunt called two jam-pots high, I was speedy. This stood me in good stead. I managed to get into the school's teams in all sports and also won individually at tennis. I loved it all, except again school dinners. As earlier, I went home at lunch time and in the summer, after eating a small meal would skip 700 times in the garden until running back to the school gates for afternoon lessons.

I won prizes for results in end of year exams until I came to school certificate and the higher level exams when I was keener on social and sporting life. Boys were not a great interest, as I was still much involved with my brother and would be thought immature today. I played tennis and hockey for the school and practised whenever I could. I took part in county tournaments but with no distinction. I had been a school prefect for a couple of years and captain of my house for longer and I was proud to be elected head prefect for my final year. I was no great favourite of my headmistress, Eileen Evans, whom I called a show off. I later learned that she and her deputy, with whom she lived, Margaret Osborn, did not wish me to be number one but were overruled by the unanimous vote of the rest of the staff and prefects. Looking back now I see myself as too lively, original and fun loving for the post the head saw as a serious one.

During that year I got together a team of prefects who worked well together and had new ideas about their role in the school of which staff and pupils approved. The head did not like me which made things a bit tricky at times. Admittedly I did not conform to her image and did some naughty things which were great fun.

One was during the very cold winter of 1951-52 when the static water tank at the school, a remnant left from the fire fighting in the war, froze over. It had sloping sides and was half full of water, now nearly solid. It was easy to get into the school grounds as the railings around it had to be taken down for armaments during the war. I climbed into school and, in the dark, skated on the water tank.

Every morning after assembly, which I called a hymn, a prayer and a ticking off, the head gave announcements. "I wish to see anyone who has knowledge of someone skating on the water tank last night" she enquired. Then a long explanation of how dangerous it was. It probably was, but I was happy to take that risk, and was a sensible person.

One of my tasks as head girl was to see the headmistress for instructions daily after assembly. So it was that I met with Mrs Evans next morning after my skating spree which my parents took in their stride. I listened to her instructions for the day, got as far as her office door, and, with one hand on the doorknob said, "By the way. I was skating on the water tank last night." Out of the door like lightning. I don't recall if there were any later repercussions – she probably had had enough of me by then.

On another occasion I had a merry wheeze on April Fool's Day. I took the key out of its place in the staff room door, and when everyone, pupils and staff were at morning break, I locked the staff in, so giving us an extra long play. (No wonder I was popular with the girls) We watched through the playground windows as staff tried to turn the door handle. After about 20 minutes extra play I sneaked in, turned the key, and fled. We loved it, the teachers came out as if nothing had happened, and nothing further was said. I suppose they might have felt they had been made a Fool of.

My school reports always included the words lively and enthusiastic. Whether that was commendable I am not sure.

I think that I was naughty, but the naughtiness always had some humour in it, and was never cruel. However, I did plot one April Fool which could be thought unkind if not familiar with the friend who was my victim. Sheila and I were great buddies. She made fun of me, - titch and she was kipper-feet. She certainly had flat feet. For April Fool's Day I put a kipper in each of her gym shoes, boxed them up and posted them to her. By the time the postman delivered them they were pretty high.

Digging in the sand aged 12

"I'll get you" was her response, but she was not angry. Revenge came quickly. I had very long plaits. On the way home together she dragged me, by my plaits, past my house and out of sight of my home. There she tied me to a lamp post by my own hair, the plaits being long enough to go round the lamp post. She then went on her way. I was stuck, not able to get to my hair knotted out of reach. After some time, our coalman came along on his bicycle. With great amusement he untied me as I told him the tale. "Don't tell my mother please." And he never did, but always gave me a wink when he delivered the coal. During my sixth form years of course, I had my future to think of. My brother had just started at St George's Medical School in London, and so when I said I was thinking of medicine or veterinary medicine both home and school thought I was influenced by brother Hugh. In fact, long before this time I had felt that this was what I needed to do. I had found I could keep calm in a crisis, probably starting with the bomb next to my infants school. Another occasion was when aged about 12 I took charge when my mother had an accident. This was just post-war, and we had no refrigerator, so our milk was kept cool in the air raid shelter. On a sunny autumn morning the french doors in the dining room were open as we started breakfast. It was only when we heard a low groaning that we realised that Mummy was not with us and that the sound came from the garden. We found her barely conscious, by a corner of the house where she had slipped on the damp ground whilst carrying the glass milk bottle. She was bleeding heavily from a two inch gash on her forehead. Daddy and Hugh carried her into an armchair and I collected water and towel to clean up the wound. As I did this and tried to revive my mother, I suggested to father that he went to use a neighbour's phone, since we did not have one. In his authoritative schoolmasterly manner, he said, "Wait a minute, wait a minute," and passed out in the other armchair. Whom to revive first? I realised brother Hugh was nowhere to be seen. I found him holding his head halfway up the stairs! I ordered him to get the doctor by calling on the neighbour's phone as I went back to the two fainting parents. With some pressure I had managed to stem the flow of blood from the head wound by the time our neighbour arrived with news that the doctor, the same dear man who had dealt with my birth saga, was on his way. Looking at our parents lying barely conscious, one with a head wound, our neighbour thought it was either a suicide pact or what is now termed a domestic. I watched Dr Robertson suture the wound and questioned him about catgut. He was amused at my interest.

So, I had had experience of a kind when I told my father of my career ideas. Vet or doctor? "Well Jan" he said with a twinkle in his eye, "the choice must be made. Could you give an enema to an elephant?" I was small for my age, hence my decision to become a doctor was made.

During my teenage years I was becoming more aware of the friction between my parents. My father was a schoolmaster through and through, and my mother frustrated academically by the misfortunes of her young life which deprived her of the future education she deserved. I shall write something of her story and that of her mother, my grandmother. Their personalities were different and my mother, although, like father, she had a good sense of humour, she tended to pessimism and was a grumbler. Whether because of my arrival in the world resulting in her fight for life with puerperal sepsis or the fact that I had the educational advantages she never had, I do not know. But I do know that there was never a mother/daughter relationship which I longed for. In some ways she was indeed unkind to me. It was decades later that I reflected on her attention seeking whenever I achieved at school. The prime example of this was when I was awarded a school prize on Speech Day, she would distract attention by fainting and being helped out of the hall. No adulation ever came to me, but I was asked, "How is your poor mother?"

Learning From the Past

I pause here to reflect on my mother's young life, which was the stuff of novels.

Understanding what had been before gives insight into our relationship so long afterwards. Her mother, Martha Hearn, known as Patty, was very pretty and well known in Luton for her looks. Like many women in the town at the turn of the century she was employed in the hat industry. Luton, in South Bedfordshire was surrounded by farming. Straw was in abundance and so supplied the straw hat trade. Plaited straw for boaters and bonnets was always in demand. Indeed, for all his life French idol Maurice Chevalier was supplied with his signature boater by one hat factory in the town.

Martha, my grandmother came from a devout Christian family, very much involved in the local congregational chapel. So her marriage to a popular footballer was unexpected. Their life reads like a Cookson novel but not with a happy ending.

Hugh Galbraith was a very talented footballer, known as Shoot Gallie, Shoot. In 1895 at the age of 26 he arrived at Luton Station where he was met by the mayor and other dignitaries. He was a Scot who had first played for his home town Dundee. Walking from the station he spotted Martha Hearn across the road and asked her name. "I'll marry her," he is reputed to have said. Three years later he did. All was well initially. He was fêted in the town the more goals he scored. Son Alfred was born in 1900 and my mother Marjorie in 1902. Their lifestyle was that of today's soccer celebrities. Mummy remembered the nanny, the nursery and the rocking horse. However, all was not well. Martha was still devoted to her chapel. She was no companion to her husband who gradually drank to excess and was flattered by the attention of wealthy friends, who introduced him to horse racing and gambling. His health suffered and he developed crippling arthritis. At home the children and their mother waited for father to come home after matches knowing he may be the worse for wear. Baby number three Harold was born and doted on by his father. He was a very pretty baby. At 3 years old he died from diphtheria. Hugh could not cope and with his drinking came violence. Mummy recalled how all knives were hidden before he came home.

All this coincided with his retirement from his successful soccer career. He was a sensational forward holding the town record goal scoring for over 20 years. In retirement he had a hat factory but still spent money gambling recklessly, until eventually he lost the hat business and with his deteriorating health became unable to support his family. By the outbreak of the first world war the marriage had broken down. Elder son, Alfred was apprenticed to Handley-Page Aircraft Engineers at Hendon. Misfortune again struck. As soon as he was able he learned to fly and gained his officer's wings in the newly created Royal Flying Corp. At 18 in 1918 he was sent out to Egypt and in Mesopotamia he was killed. How? We do not know. Was it a flying accident or some other tragedy? So the First World War brought a further bereavement to the family.

Mummy and my grandmother by this time had turned to their chapel for support and were given accommodation by their minister and his wife. Hugh Galbraith, my sporting grandfather, was never spoken of. He died in 1930. The same year that my parents married. It must have been a time of turmoil of emotions from which both my mother and grandmother never recovered. Knowing this history does give me some insight into my mother's character and behaviour.

1953

Off to Bart's

When things were getting too much for her, Mummy would take to her bed, and I would be in charge from my early teens. She had a fraught relationship with her mother. Their personalities were similar. I was 17 when my grandmother died. My mother in her bereavement I think experienced guilt for the way in which she had behaved. I was victim of her unhappiness, as indeed was my father. At the time when I left school as head girl and was accepted as a medical student at Bart's Hospital in the City of London, mother went into a decline. A physical manifestation of her bereavement.

In the first term at St Bartholomew's Hospital to study First MB, I travelled daily from Luton to St Pancras. On my evening return I would have to prepare supper, do my studies and get ready for the next day. It was not easy. Mummy stayed in bed for much of this time with no specific diagnosis. My brother, by then a clinical student at St George's Hospital was much involved with Erica Cleaver, the daughter of a local family friend. She had just come down from university in Leeds. Her mother and mine had been friends for some time and sang and played together in local entertainments. Hugh asked me if I thought he should marry Erica. I was both flattered and surprised for him to ask, but we were close and shared much, especially as we knew things at home were not so happy. I said Hugh must decide for himself, but that I would be happy with his choice. So it was that Hugh and Erica became engaged. Erica had a job in London at the Geological Survey at the Natural History Museum, which entailed measuring the depth of wells in the Thames Valley. The office was called The Water Cart. Hugh was just qualifying and had a post of houseman at St George's Hospital.

I was accepted at Bart's in 1953, soon after the coronation of Elizabeth II.

Off to Bart's aged 19

Very different circumstances from today. In my admission year, were 60 men and 4 women. Most of those admitted came from public school and were alien to my experience at a state high school. However, I seemed to be accepted by my year and had many friends, among them my first serious boyfriend, John.

A product of Uppingham School he had good manners and was well spoken, despite a slight stammer, which worried him more than others. He was a gentle and caring consort. I was more gregarious and enjoyed the company of my fellow students. At the time of my admission for First MB I was much in need of further tuition for both chemistry and physics, which I had only started in sixth form of my High School. I was more than fortunate to have as professor of physics Polish Joseph Rotblat, who was an instigator of the movement of Pugwash, the scientists against atomic weapon development. Fleeing from Poland he had been working in the States in the war on the development of the atomic bomb. Having been appalled at the destruction of Hiroshima and Nagasaki, he then devoted his life to development of nuclear medicine and was centred at Bart's. A dear man who was much admired by his students until his death in 2005 in his 90s. We all rejoiced when he shared in the Nobel Peace Prize in 1995. To be taught physics by him gave meaning and purpose to the subject which had troubled me previously.

My preclinical years were spent at the Medical College in Charterhouse Square in close proximity to the Carthusian Monastery buildings from which it got its name. Bart's, a wealthy hospital had been on the same site by Smithfield Meat Market in the City since its establishment by Rahere as a hospice in 1123. Rahere was court jester to Henry I, and, returning with the king from the Crusade, he fell sick with malaria in Italy. Being nigh unto death he prayed for deliverance and asked God what he should do in gratitude. He had a vision in which he was told to return to London and found a hospice in the name of St Bartholomew in Smith's Field. Thus, Bart's was established and became renowned. It has two churches, one inside the hospital walls, Bart's the Less and the famous Bart's the Great just outside the walls. The latter was a large monastic church until the Reformation. Today it is still very beautiful and a tourist attraction in the city. Very popular for society weddings. It was used in the film Four Weddings and a Funeral.

Whilst I was a student, I would often worship at evensong in Bart's the Great, where the music was wonderful. The organist and choir master was Paul Steinitz, who later founded the Bach choir. It was marvellous to listen to this small choir of professional singers as they sang a Bach cantata every Sunday evening. A group of us who loved singing were inspired by the choir and would go back to College Hall in Charterhouse Square and continue singing in the music room. In later years some of us would make a group who wrote and sang material, in the Christmas shows we put on at Bart's. We also sang for our supper at debutantes balls. These were for the wealthy young women who would be presented at Court that year. All this ended shortly after our days taking part.

I was a mediocre student, looking back, mostly because I enjoyed life so much that studying became the means to an end to stay at Bart's where I was so happy. Sport played a large part in life. Despite our limited number, Bart's women's hockey team was formidable, winning the Hospital Cup for 7 years. I played left wing. The friendships made then remained long after, as too with the tennis team in the summer months. Every Saturday we travelled by train to the Hospital sports field at Chislehurst to play matches with sides from around London and beyond. The boys teams for rugger and football also were on site, so there was much socialising after the matches, and we all came back together to College Hall in the evening. I remember taking on a bet that I couldn't carry the rugger captain, 6ft and 15 stone back from Aldersgate Station to the Hall – about 350 yds. They reckoned a 5ft weakling like me, would not take up the challenge. I did, much to the hilarity of all of us. I was always game for a lark and had such fun doing daft things. For example, how many could get in a telephone box? or how many could stand on the international post box in Charterhouse Square? These ridiculous things are still more memorable to me than the lectures, lab sessions and dissection in the anatomy room, although the latter was always my favourite.

Following the preclinical exams in 1956 I was a white coated, stethoscoped student on the wards in the Hospital. None of us would have hung stethoscopes round our necks in those days. Formality was part of the learning curve for the days to come when we were qualified. Dress mattered and all the men wore ties and suits or sports jackets. We respected the consultants who taught us on ward rounds, and the film Doctor in the House which came out about that time rang true on many occasions. Richard Gordon, the author, was a Bart's Man and he had been an anaesthetist in the hospital before I arrived. There was rivalry between the London Hospitals. Rag Days gave an excuse to raid other medical schools. e.g. Guys, St Thomas, the London, UCH and St Marys, usually to steal their mascot. Ours, Percy was an ugly brute like a Red Indian totem pole in Bart's colours of black and white.

One year the Dean's son, a rather wet gentleman, was captured by Tommies, and turned out in Piccadilly Circus at rush hour, sans pants, with white feathers glued to his behind. These days we would all be breathalysed, tested for drugs and land up in clink. Then the splendid, very tall City policemen just knew us all and sent us on our way. Violence never came into our frivolity and the police seemed more amused than angry. Indeed, on one occasion after a particularly exciting Rugger Cup match was being celebrated in our local the White Hart the police suggested we went round to their bar at Snow Hill Police Station when the pubs shut. How life has changed.

As a clinical student living in College Hall Charterhouse Square, one shared life on a daily basis with about 60 other students. Bart's was ahead of its time, when one thinks of the segregation of the sexes at Oxbridge, for we had five floors for the men, and the top floor, with balconies, for the women. We therefore had a good social life with visits to theatres, concerts and cinemas always possible with a male escort. As well as times of study there was much hilarity and horseplay. I seemed to be involved in much of this among the boys of my year and above. One memorable jape started when I was woken from sleep at about midnight and became aware of the door opening and, in the moonlight, I saw a gorilla enter the room. I sat up in bed and yelled my head off. The apparition disappeared and girls from rooms around came to find the cause of the commotion. Only next morning did one of the most charming men in my year, whose room was on the floor below mine, come to apologise for scaring me, saying he had not reckoned with me being fast asleep. "I'll get you Colin" I warned with a laugh. Get him indeed I did. Shortly afterwards I saw from my balcony that the gorilla was off to play squash. Quickly I went to his room and took every pair of trousers he possessed down to his rugger shorts. I had a large dress box which had contained my dress for the Bart's Ball later that month. In went the trousers, off to the principal London GPO round the corner. I had addressed the box to his fiancée who lived in the Nurses Home at the hospital. I was back in my room before the game of squash was finished. At supper that evening, wearing borrowed trousers, he asked if I had his. In all honesty I could say I had not. And so, it continued for 36 hours until his fiancée opened her parcel. We agreed, gorilla and I, that we were quits and remained good friends.

Another laugh came when the beefy rugger boys carried an Austin 7 into the College Hall and left it outside the lift. A bit cruel really, but fun to hear about. The owner was a devoted young man from another college who visited his girlfriend, who lived on the sixth floor, most evenings. He would not say boo to a goose and never spoke to any of us but hurried away like a scared rabbit each visit. Well he might, for when he came out of the lift he was confronted by his Austin 7. After a suitable delay, the boys did the decent thing and carried it outside once more.

I loved everything about the clinical years at Bart's except pathology. I just could not cope with pathology exams and this became a millstone round my neck. When in finals I managed to pass everything except the repeat exam in pathology. My response to this was to make my way to the Apothecaries Hall in Blackfriars Lane and sign up to take their next exams for the qualification LMSSA. As well as pathology there were papers in forensic medicine and public health, not forgetting medicine, surgery and obstetrics and gynaecology of the London MB. Since money was in short supply, I took my qualification for preregistration in order to get my first job.

Perhaps I had too much fun as a student, but in my ancient days I do not regret that. The memories far exceed any I might have of exams passed.

I did a lot of acting whilst a clinical student and wrote and performed in many Christmas ward shows, the best items of which were put on in review at the Cripplegate Theatre for a week. I loved these performances and the audience seemed to love them too. One Christmas I was a singing and dancing cat in our version of Dick Whittington. It was the time of Bill Hayley and the Comets and I did a great jive with one of the boys to Rock Around the Clock.

Before I left Bart's I was awarded a very lucrative prize, 'the Heyward Prize' for my contribution to the Students Union of the Medical School.

1959

I Am Dr Swallow

And so – What now doctor?

I arrived home to my parents, Dr Swallow no 2 just before Christmas 1959.

My brother Hugh, a GP in the town, was at home with mumps, a more serious infectious illness in adults than children. A further problem for the family was that my sister-in-law, Erica, was expecting their second child any time soon. Their first child, Nicholas has been born on January 2nd that year and the expected date for baby no 2 was uncertain. I moved in to help look after Nick and give Erica some rest. My brother recovered enough to return to practice 10 days before Christmas.

Two memorable happenings stay with me from that time. I am uncertain of the order in which they came, but both will not be forgotten.

I had been appointed as a Casualty Officer at the Luton and Dunstable Hospital to start on January 1st, 1960. In December 1959, whilst staying with my brother and sister-in-law as nanny I was called by the hospital asking if I could do a 5-11 p.m. session for them as the doctor I was due to replace in January was unwell. I duly arrived in Casualty as the Nurse in Charge Sister Wood was chatting with the consultant Laurie Plewes as they prepared to go off duty.

Mummy and Daddy

"I see Denis Bridges is at large" said Woody. "Funny if he turned up here." To which Mr Plewes agreed. I was introduced all round and went up to the doctors mess for supper. As we sat down it seemed all the bells in heaven were ringing as an ambulance drove into the reception area below us. I was called down at once and asked to see the casualty in the ambulance. There I found a young man about 20 years of age shouting, "Don't cut it off, don't cut it off, it's only broken!"

I knew enough to know that we should bring him into the hospital casualty ward. It was there we could see his right foot was severed and only held on by a tendon, the foot lying up beside his calf. This was a bit of a shock for my first patient, but worse was to come. When we removed his trousers, we found his other leg was amputated below the knee. His name? Denis Bridges.

His is a story in itself and I gradually learned it as we prepared him for theatre for below knee amputation of his other leg. By this time police were in action and the explanation to how this had happened began to emerge.

Denis Bridges came from a gypsy family who had connections with a part of Luton, Leagrave. He had been in trouble with the police during his teenage years. So much so, that on one occasion as they searched for him, he came to his grandmother's house by the railway line in Leagrave to escape arrest. As police came to the house, Denis ran down to the end of the garden and climbed over onto the railway line. What happened next is unclear, but it resulted in Denis's left foot being run over by a train, and subsequently the first amputation.

Of course, this made local, and later, national news as Denis told the story that he had been trying to save a dog on the line and got his foot caught. How much of this is true I do not know. I do know that a financial reward for his bravery ensued.

We now know that he squandered that money and indulged in those teenage years in a life of petty crime.

When we pick up the tale again Denis was in Bedford Gaol awaiting sentence for receiving a stolen rifle. He said his artificial limb was hurting and was taken to the local hospital. He then escaped by climbing out of a lavatory window and disappearing. The search was on for Denis Bridges once more. What happened next is extraordinary. Did Denis think "it worked once, it will work again"? He went to grandmother's house. The police appeared. He climbed onto the railway line and stuck his other foot under a train. My first patient in Casualty. Never to be forgotten. Denis had officers by his bedside as he recovered from amputation number two and then was removed to Wormwood Scrubs.

So much for my introduction to my chosen profession. Meanwhile, at my brother's flat Christmas preparations were beginning whilst I helped care for the 11-month-old Nicholas. On December 21st I asked Erica if she wanted to have the baby that year or the next, since no date was known. She opted for the week to come. I bought a bottle of castor oil and gave her, what I know now, was a large dose. As we washed up after lunch, she said the castor oil would at least cure her constipation and disappeared to the lavatory. Time passed and putting my head round the door I found her still there. I laid a hand on her abdomen and without comment realised she was in labour, although so soon after the first birth she seemed unaware. I sprinted Nick in his pram to Granny down the road and rushed back to suggest to Erica that a call to the midwife, GP and or Hugh was advisable. No replies, just messages that Erica was in labour left with everyone. Meanwhile the planned home delivery in Nicky's nursery was to be organised. I made up the bed and made Erica comfortable. The small kitchen table was to be dismantled and moved in for the midwife's needs. Suffice it to say that I only had 3 legs off the table before Erica said she wanted to push. I had left the front door open and was just delivering the baby when I heard the midwife arriving. As she heard the baby cry, she said, "I won't bring up the gas and air machine." I handed over to her thankfully to cut the cord and deliver the placenta.

Sarah Jane Swallow had arrived. That Christmas was a hectic one for me, looking after Nicky, Erica, making mince pies at midnight and cooking a full Christmas dinner for us to have together on Christmas evening, tired though we were.

My A&E, or Casualty as it was called in the 60s, appointment started in January 1960. It was a good starting post at the Luton & Dunstable Hospital where accidents abounded in the days of no crash helmets and variable speed limits. For me it was a good eye-opener to the public's use of the NHS, or abuse of the NHS. For example on a Sunday afternoon outing, "We've just brought my mum in for you to cut her toenails." Not unusual misuse of professional time. As well as working in A&E I had an orthopaedic ward to look after and assisting Mr Plewes in theatre. He was a remarkable Canadian who had started a Rehabilitation Unit for men at Vauxhall Motors, getting them back to work quickly after injury.

He was a very fair boss and realised housemen had a tough time working very long hours. For example, I was on my own in this busy department every other weekend from Friday lunchtime until Monday morning. This included night duty. I could then have Monday afternoon off. Hooray!

The Hospital was close to the M1, A5 and A6 and so accident work was always ongoing. One very windy weekend three ambulances arrived simultaneously. I admitted the three casualties. "What has happened to you?" Answer, "I fell off a camel at Whipsnade Zoo." No 2 Same question. Answer, "I was blown out of my husband's motorbike side car on the M1." No 3, Same question. Answer, "I crashed my glider on Dunstable Downs."

As I went from one cubicle to the next, I found myself getting them muddled. Time for a laugh and get on with the job. I met all sorts. Having just completed a busy evening at 11.30 p.m., as always, on my own, the hospital telephonist called, "Don't go to bed, they're bringing in an M1 crash."

About midnight three injured Chinamen arrived, shocked and moaning, "Paing, paing, paing." Not a word of english and no interpreter. One did all the clerical work as well as diagnosis and treatment. I labelled them Ping 1, Ping 2 and Ping 3 all on their wrists. One had a fractured humerus. Two had lacerations and a fractured clavicle. But Three had no apparent injury initially but moaned, "Paing, paing, paing." As we monitored his condition it was apparent that he had internal abdominal injury. The surgical team took him to theatre and removed a ruptured spleen.

It was only next morning as I came on the ward at 8.30 a.m. that sister asked, "Were you on last night? Who was with you?" "No-one, why?" She took from the desk drawer, knuckle dusters and flick knives, taken off our Chinamen. Police explained they were part of a Triad making their way back to London. I'm glad I didn't know.

It was good to be part of a hospital team who enjoyed working together and helped each other whenever we could. Camaraderie of the best kind.

I very much missed that in my next six-month post at the Luton & Dunstable children's hospital. This was a Victorian building across the town from the main hospital having two wards and a small neonatal ward, a theatre and outpatient department. The greatest difficulty was that it was very lonely. The only other resident staff member was a woman paediatric registrar who was a bitter misfit, having been turned down for many posts. However hard I worked she always found fault. Despite my love of the patients, she certainly put me off paediatrics, as also did the consultant for whom we worked. I found him idle and disinterested. He left me with an enormous amount of responsibility when only qualified for six months. With only a nurse to assist

I was expected to do total exchange transfusion on tiny rhesus babies within their first day of life, often throughout the night. How things have changed. I was charged to get down the waiting list for circumcisions. These were done each week on a table in a room off one of the wards. Open ether on a mask was administered by one of the local GPs. Not for nothing did one of the sisters call me the Circumcision Queen. When asking a mother why it was being done it was not unusual to have the answer, "Well next door's boy has been done" or "I thought he had to". The rabbi did those performed for religious reasons and no doctors were involved. A sharpened long thumbnail did the trick soon after birth.

We also had to get down the massive waiting list for tonsils and adenoids. These were also done in the room off the ward and were a lucrative perk for two local GPs. I'm glad to say we did not have a serious bleed in the six months I was there.

Pathology and haematology were, by present standards primitive. Diagnosis of leukaemia was more difficult than today. I will tell later of one 10-year-old girl who was in the ward for all my time as a houseman. She came from a complex family where her mother, divorced and remarried an eighteen-year-old in the time the little girl was on the ward. She was an only child.

The most significant episodes of my six months were the arrival of new-born babies described by one old Scottish lady doctor in the town as not quite finished off. These were the first we had seen of the thalidomide babies. The drug, under the name of Distaval was used in pregnancy to help in morning sickness with good effect. It was only after the birth that the malformities of limbs were seen and the connection made. Little deformed hands coming out of the shoulder girdle or a tibia or fibula from the pelvis were very distressing to see. The parents were in shock and overwrought. Scanning in pregnancy had not been established as it is today. My consultant, as described before, was a sharp contrast to the dynamic Canadian Laurie Plewes, for whom I worked in A&E. When I said how distressing it was to take in these deformed babies and asked if he had seen a lot over the years, his reply was, "It does happen." No concern or curiosity.

I was pleased to leave paediatrics and take a post as Senior House Officer at Lincoln. A long way from home ground and very hard work. My responsibility was for male and female general medical wards. Each had 25 beds and also a further chest ward of the same mixed number. I had to take all the bloods daily and clerk every patient. Haematology involved fierce large steel needles and glass syringes, all needing sterilisation at the end of the collection. I started the job in a snowy January. The hospital, single storey, had been built in the war for the American Air Force. The main corridor, in some places open to the elements, was ¼ mile long up a hillside. I had wards at both ends of the corridor. I lived with all male colleagues, a Pole, an Indian, a Pakistani and my New Zealand registrar in an ex-Service quarter, where the walls were bare breeze block. After some months I succumbed to glandular fever and was sent home for 4 weeks recuperation. I was exhausted.

Much happier times however followed. I was appointed as a Junior Registrar in General Practice back at my teaching hospital Bart's. In those days, the fact that general practice needed special skills was not recognised and doctors started as GPs once they were registered with the General Medical Council. Bart's however acknowledged the varied experience needed for general practice. Posts funded by the medical college were created in which those appointed planned their own programmes of work according to what they considered they would need in general practice. One approached the consultant with whom you wished to work, and he would take you under his wing and teach you for the time you felt appropriate. Three-month sessions were mostly taken. I did ENT, skins, eyes, psychiatry. Also anaesthetics, useful for A&E work. It was a wonderful experience in the hospital I so much loved and I was, at last, among friends. I shared a flat off Haverstock Hill in Hampstead with two clinical students, one of whom was starry eyed and engaged to a fellow student in her year. My memory of him is of bouncing in like Tigger, going to the fridge and helping himself to anything he fancied. No offer of payment at any time. I was not short of male escorts and being back in London gave scope for a delightful social life, especially enjoying concerts and theatre. I still have a collection of theatre programmes, many from that time in 1962-63. It was also a blessed relief to have no night duty and not be answerable to a consultant. I learned so much in those two years which I know stood me in good stead in the years to come.

I had now some good experience under my belt but had

done no midwifery and gynaecology since qualifying. At Bart's these posts, as senior house officers, had always gone to a chosen few men, particularly for the senior consultant, John Beattie, JB. He was a very wealthy man who exuded an air of supremacy, even in height, being well over 6 foot. He arrived at the hospital in either a Lagonda or Bentley, chauffeur driven. It had been traditional that, because JB was president of Bart's rugby club, the team captain would expect to have the job for him in the bag. There had never been a woman appointed to this post for the senior consultant. So it was as a challenge from some of my colleagues that I applied for his SHO position. It was also traditional at Bart's that one asked the consultant personally in hope of a favourable answer. It was quite a surprise to me when I plucked up courage to ask if I might apply, that he replied, "I'd be delighted."

So began another year of experience I remember with pleasure, hard work though it was. First, six months of gynaecology to be followed by midwifery.

JB was a showman and took great amusement from the difference in height between us. I was just about five foot tall. "Where is she?" he would ask. "I'm under your left armpit Sir." Wry smiles from his student audience.

Ward rounds each week were his time to show off to the students. Little did they know what had gone before to enable him to perform. All patients were admitted the day before this round and had to be clerked and examined by me and all notes ready for sister's trolley to accompany the parade to each bed. It was not enough for JB that I had written a précis of each patient's history and examination. He also had to have a nugget of nonsense of some kind for each one. Then, when asking a student for a history he would give the impression that he knew so much about each patient. It was usually a woman student that he would tease in this way. I remember one very earnest girl who had given an excellent report only to hear, "And what about the dalmatians?" Poor girl, her face said it all. "You didn't find out about her dogs? Who is going to look after them if she is here for ten days?" A lecture then to all about knowing more than just the clinical findings. Not exactly holistic medicine but something for them to think about. John Beattie treated me well and I worked hard for him. He was responsible for the sewing room making me small white theatre suits for me to wear under the surgical gowns. He trusted me enough to change places with me and he assisted whilst I did a hysterectomy in the final weeks of my post.

It was during this time at Bart's that I was called to see once more the little girl with leukaemia I had known at the children's hospital in Luton over three years earlier. In fact, she had been a favourite of mine and apparently, I was of hers. Whilst working in Lincoln I had a letter from her telling me that she was to be christened and asking my permission to be named Jan after me. Very humbling. Even more so was to come when at Bart's I was given a note by a porter as I came out of the gynae theatre. It was a request from this little girl that I go to see her, now in the Royal Marsden Hospital in London. Somehow, she had tracked me down and asked the staff there to find me.

It so happened that I had an afternoon off and went at once to see her.

This was one of the most heart-breaking experiences I have ever had.

She was in an adult ward and had several staff at her bedside. As I approached, I could see that she was bleeding from nose and mouth and ashen in colour. Despite this when she saw me, she said, almost as a reassurance to the nurses, "Here's Jan, she's come, she'll know what to do." Never had I felt so sad and so helpless.

Jan died the next day, aged nearly 14 years.

The midwifery post was enjoyable but often, I felt, unsatisfactory. There was a lack of sensitivity to what women about to give birth might be feeling. Little reassurance to the apprehensive, and in some cases ignorance of what to expect of labour. Most women came from the local area of Clerkenwell and beyond. Many from deprived homes. They were grateful for any service the hospital could offer them. The National Health Service remember was only fifteen years old, truly in its infancy.

Some consultants used the service, or, we would say today, abused the service by admitting any of their private patients whom they considered may need more expertise in their delivery than their private hospitals might give. This was very difficult for me. I disliked being used in this way and felt it was dishonest of the consultants who were charging high fees but expecting our co-operation.

Two particular experiences spring to mind in this regard.

One involved the labour of such a private patient of her first child. Tragically we had had to break the news to her and her husband that there was no sign of life in this final stage of pregnancy and she was admitted to deliver a dead baby.

One difficulty for all staff concerned was that the labour ward consisted of two beds separated only by a curtain. It was inevitable that each mother was aware of the other.

At the time when this poor girl was delivering her dead baby, admitted to the bed the other side of the curtain was a hysterical young Italian girl who had come in off the street in labour. She had had no antenatal care and was unaware of her pregnancy until brought into Bart's by her equally hysterical mother.

As I tried to calm her and give her instructions over the shouting and tears of her delivery, I was constantly aware of the stoical silence from the next bed of the patient being delivered of a dead child. Only the duty midwife was with her. Partners were not considered to be a necessary support in those days.

John Beattie had a prosperous obstetric clientele, but as he neared retirement he no longer wished to deal with these confinements, however lucrative they might be. His answer was to double his fees, hoping to put off a number of clients. Instead, the mentality of many being, the more expensive, the better the service, he in fact doubled his list, much to his chagrin. His solution was to hand over the whole list to the 'junior' third consultant, Gordon Bourne. Gordon delighted in this new found wealth and enjoyed arriving in the Square at Bart's in his Jaguar. He was very different from JB and I did not enjoy working for him. He too had this arrangement of admitting his private patients into Bart's all NHS beds.

So it was that when his private patient was admitted in early labour, I did as his notes instructed, and rang his home number. His wife took the message. It was a busy night and I had had no sleep when, in the early hours I was informed that the baby was successfully delivered but there was no sign of the placenta. A retained placenta is a hazard of midwifery and can lead to complications. It is important to manually remove it under general anaesthetic as soon as possible.

Since Gordon Bourne's notes said to inform of the progress I rang him as soon as possible only once more to be told that he was not available but would be contacted. My only solution was to discuss the problem with his registrar, who was in the hospital but involved elsewhere. He gave me instruction to go ahead and do the manual removal. I did this and all was well by the time Gordon Bourne swept into the Square four hours later. He sent for me. "Who did this manual removal?" "I did." "Why wasn't I informed?" "You were sir, at all stages of delivery." "If I had known you were to let her deliver whilst you were tucked up in your little bed, I would have come in and delivered her myself." At this I saw red and verbally exploded. "And that's exactly what you should have done. If I am expected to deal with your private patients, you must accept the consequences.

I informed you all along as instructed but couldn't wait for an answer. I did as instructed by your registrar!" Oh! What have I done? It was unheard of to lose one's temper with a consultant. I swept out of his office before he could reply. I awaited my dismissal for insubordination. However, nothing happened. When I was about to go into theatre with JB two days later he said to me, "I hear you had a set to with Gordon?" Here it comes I thought. Time to pack my bags. John Beattie said he had discussed this with Gordon and to my surprise was told that Gordon had said, "She's right you know." I respected him for this remark. I breathed a sigh of relief and finished the post with glowing references from JB.

So, what now? My time at Bart's was ended and I was to look for fresh fields and pastures new. But where?

Life is full of coincidences or as one of my friends calls it 'God's little surprises'. I have mentioned the fiancé of my Hampstead medical student flat mate previously. It so happened that a tragedy had struck the fiancé's family at this time. His doctor father, mother and three young siblings were on the ferry for a holiday in Ireland when father had a heart attack and died. Not only was this heart-breaking for the family but also for father's practice at Freshwater on the Isle of Wight. The town was left without a doctor. Robin, the boyfriend knew I had just finished my time at Bart's and asked if I would be willing to do a locum until a new partner was found for the practice of three covering the west of the Island. So my first GP post arrived without planning and proved to be an educating and amusing three months.

Not much of what I had learned at medical school seemed relevant but I learned so much about the arts of reassurance and persuasion which are part of a doctor's armamentarium. The practice, indeed, Freshwater and its environs, had never had a lady doctor before and word of mouth soon sent many to my surgery purely out of curiosity. Home visits were quite new to me and finding my way around the lanes to the remote cottages was a challenge. When I called, at last, at one such patient's home and introduced myself I was not expecting the conversation that followed. The door was opened by a middle-aged woman who said the request for a visit came from her mother, whom she called up the stairs to come forward. "What's the problem with mother?" "Oh, there's no problem, but we'd heard all about you and mother wanted to see you!" For this I had spent over an hour, driving miles.

Another time I was called at midnight to a man having an asthma attack. Being new to such calls I had left lights on in my Mini and when I went to leave at 2.00 a.m. my battery was flat. In the car I had a large bag of equipment, plus a midwifery bag. How to get home with this load? Walking about ½ mile was the only possibility. In the 3 months I had been in Freshwater I had had no sign of the constabulary. So it was a surprise, when having struggled 100 yards a police car pulled up beside me. As the window was lowered, I cried, "Oh, you're the answer to a maiden's prayer!" to the fresh-faced young policeman at the wheel. He blushed and looked a little confused. I think he thought I was a lady of the night going about my business. However, he kindly drove me to the home I shared with the doctor's widow in the house above the surgery.

Once again abuse of the system was common. One maiden lady visited every Monday evening surgery, simply for a regular prescription. When I suggested that she could call monthly she was aghast, adamant that she came every week. This gave insight into a side of general practice not taught in medical school. The rôle of the doctor in a community such as that at Freshwater. Everyone I saw spoke so warmly of Dr Knill Jones whose death in his forties was felt deeply by his patients. He had been their friend, counsellor and confessor as well as tending to their physical needs for so many years, and his loss was a bereavement for them all. Use of the telephone was also an unusual requirement for many. I had a call after midnight, "Come quick, Rose Cottage." Phone put down. I woke Jocelyn Knill Jones, only to hear that there were about five Rose Cottages on the practice. The phone rang again. "He hasn't come, he hasn't come." This time I was able to quickly get the address and wend my way to the tiny cottage where sadly the patient was in extremis, or, what his overwrought wife described as "All blood and corruption!" He was someone who didn't believe in doctors and had avoided the surgery. It was too late to save this man, whom I suspect had a carcinoma of the stomach.

I have just one piece of visible evidence from my time at Freshwater. A dear man whom I saw often said he would like to give me a leaving present, but it would take some time. He was a farrier and made me a beautiful pair of bellows which are in use to this day. Leather and brass work must have taken some days. A treasured gift.

Bellows

1964

I Run Away to Sea

My time on the Island was over and I moved to a GP locum in an all women practice in Cambridge. I was to fill in for a partner on maternity leave. There was some pressure to join the practice. After some weeks looking after dotty dons and intense mothers with clever children. I knew it was not for me. But where next? Serendipity is a lovely word and much to my liking, for it answered my question. On calling into the practice office one morning I found the British Medical Journal open at the jobs vacant page. 'Wanted for British India Steam Navigation Company School Ships, an Assistant Surgeon.' I was, within the week at the head offices of British India, no 1 Leadenhall Street, London. After interview from personnel and medical supremos I was heading for a naval tailor to be fitted out with my uniform. Miller, Rayner and Heysome were more used to measuring officers inside legs than bust sizes and the little tailor who dealt with me obviously found it all too much for him. I had to do my own measurements, of skirt and jacket size. He plucked up courage to measure arm length and then fitted me out with a tricorn hat with BI badge, shirts with detached stiff collar and black tie. I was to join the ship M.V. Devonia at Tilbury in one week's time. My tailor assured me skirt and jacket would be brought down to the docks at that time. After a frantic week of preparation, including selling my car, I was driven to Tilbury in a rainstorm by my sister-in-law,

Erica. My parents were, I think, bemused by my decision to run away to sea.

So much to learn. A completely new way of life with people I had never met. The ship was mid-stream in the Thames at Tilbury and I was taken across by ferry to be greeted at the head of the gangway by the rotund, very Scottish, purser Archie. "So you've come lassie." I said I had. I was shown to my cabin off the companion way on A deck. I liked it at once. High up bunk with drawers below, a cushioned day bed, wardrobe, desk and comfy chair. A porthole above the basin in a recess to the main area. I had collected part of the uniform – the jacket, on my way to the ship, being assured that the skirt would be brought down for me to Tilbury before sailing next day. The moment I had been waiting for, trying on my BI officer's jacket had arrived.

I was a slight figure of 5 foot tall. This jacket would have fitted Dolly Parton to a T! That evening at dinner, still in mufti, I met my fellow officers, all jolly and welcoming. Even more so when I said, "I haven't got a skirt." Cheers! "We have been waiting for you for a long time!" Next morning, I went ashore whilst the school children embarked and grabbed a paper parcel from the little tailor wandering along the quayside. "What about payment?" he asked. "I'll pay you when it fits me" I replied. Back to the cabin as the ship set sail, to try on the skirt. Would it make up for the bosomy jacket? Readers, this was in the days before the mini skirt, but on this occasion I was starting a fashion. Well above my knees. With the outsize jacket to finish off the apparition I faced the world. I had no option, knowing I could do nothing about it until we returned from my first BI Educational Cruise in ten days' time. The Senior Surgeon was most put out by the misuse of gold braid on my jacket. I was meant to have 2 and a half red and gold bands on my jacket cuffs whilst he had three. All this mattered. Rank was important. I soon learned that I was there to do the work, whilst he would socialise with passengers and open cans of Allsops beer on a regular basis. My brief was the medical care of students who came from schools all over the UK. Their Education Authorities had chartered the ship for a voyage mostly of 10-14 days duration. I had so much to discover on these Discovery Cruises. The history of the enterprise for one. BI had a remarkable Commodore, Ben Rogers, who was the Master of the Devonia. He had had a distinguished career in the Merchant Navy in the Second World War.

Before the War, Devonia's sister ship, Dunera, a troopship had taken teenage boys on educational trips in the summer holidays. These trips were mainly to the near continent. They were a great success and allowed youngsters to have a taste of life at sea, learning to live together and sharing duties on board. A retired soldier, Col. Clive Harston had been involved at that time.

After the war, BI had to find a role for the troop ships Dunera and Devonia as they were no longer in service. Col. Harston, Commodore Rogers and Tam Dalyell, a Scottish educationalist, later to be an MP, planned and launched the Educational Cruises. Any county could charter the ship and pupils would take part in voyages. A teacher came free of charge with every ten pupils. He or she was responsible for the day-to-day supervision of their party. The ship ran as a school at sea with the added experience for most pupils of living together and sleeping in dormitories. The organisation on board was excellent and one could detect the origins, both in school and army background from its founders, not to mention the notable impression of sea life given by Commodore Rogers of BI.

Medical discussion with Dr Alan Lewtas, Senior Surgeon, MV Devonia

My territory was the medical flat low in the ship. It had a consulting room, dispensary and two wards of six beds each. My patients ranged in age from 7 to 18, depending on the type of cruise. I was also involved in the care of the adult passengers, not associated with the schools, who chose to come on these cruises for the very worthwhile educational content. About 100 adults, including the teachers, would have their own facilities on the upper decks, of bars, public rooms and swimming pool. The dining room was gracious and stewarded by the Indian waiters, who were a joy. I also had a cabin steward, Abdus Salaam, who looked after me and made sure I toed the line of etiquette on board. For example, he impressed upon me that I must not be seen on deck without my tricorn hat and jacket. The jacket and skirt were by now replaced with ones that fitted. The Asian crew all came from one region in India and travelled together to join the ship in Bombay on a yearly basis. They had their own crew quarters where the smell of curry wafted in the air. Our own hospital stewards would sometimes make the two nursing sisters and myself a fish curry which was delicious. An incident with Abdus stays with me. We were about to arrive in Leningrad, one of the few western visitors to Russia in those days in the sixties. I asked Abdus if he would go ashore in the port. He closed the cabin door as he did if he was going to tell me off. This he sometimes did, behaving like a father figure. "Excuse me memsahib" he said, "You have your God topside. I have my God topside. Russia, no God topside so me not go shoreside." Topside, the uppermost part of the ship – was the region of the captain's cabin and the bridge.

The two nursing sisters who were my daily companions were wonderfully helpful at settling me into life on board. So much to learn, but so enjoyable. The daily routine for me was a morning surgery at 8.00 a.m., which lasted about 1½ hours and again at 4.00 p.m. also tending any in the sickbay and assisting the Senior Surgeon with care of the cabin passengers and crew. We were also involved in regular inspections of the galleys and crew quarters with the deck officers and were on call always for emergencies. One had to be prepared for anything and able to tackle most things. I was grateful for my Bart's training and experience in the L&D casualty department. But some challenges had no relationship to training and one resorted to common sense, ingenuity and humour. Looking after the youngest pupils on junior cruises was my favourite time. They ranged between 7 and 10 years and only took short trips of a week or so mainly to the near continent and Scandinavia. On my first time ashore we visited Oslo. I found myself on Amundsen's ship the 'Fram' where an excited group of little girls could be heard on the deck below me. Their teacher, a stern lady, was beside me. She called, "Holy Trinity, come up. Come up Holy Trinity." The only time I've heard the Trinity invoked from below!

On a rough crossing of the North Sea, a little boy whose name I recall was Oppenheimer came to morning surgery, obviously homesick. To make him feel involved I spoke of the camera hanging around his neck. "I suppose you haven't taken pictures yet?" I asked, thinking of the grey day outside. He replied, "one or two of my friends, but mostly sea." His parents were in for an exciting slide show.

One of my favourite days with the young ones was when, on opening the consulting room door, in trooped six little girls, five attending one very sad little soul. We explained that we could only see one at a time and shepherded the sad one to sit by me as the others left. I asked what the problem was. Through her tears, she took a deep breath, and in one rapid sentence said, "Well, I've got two nans and two grandpappies and the day before I came away one of my grandpappies fell off a ladder and bashed his face and I keep thinking about it all the time and I've got a cold!" I could do the cold, but what about grandpappy's bashed face? "Have you read Pollyanna?" I asked. "No Miss." I explained that Pollyanna had a difficult great aunt to whom she took beef broth and calves' foot jelly. Whichever she took, aunt was not happy. So, Pollyanna played the glad game, finding something to be glad about each day. "Now I know your Grandpappy wouldn't want you to be upset, so you come and see me tomorrow and tell me what you have been glad about today." Not something you learn from textbooks. Next morning, the queue outside the surgery was twice as long, and at the front my Pollyanna pupil. Surgery door opened and in came about 20 girls. "I said yesterday I can only see one at a time."

"Oh but" said a very cheery Pollyanna, "I went back to my dorm and told them about the glad game, so we've all come to tell you what we were glad about yesterday!" I danced with a boy. We had fish and chips, my favourite. I won the writing competition etc.

Enjoyment for passengers at sea much depends on the weather. Likewise for the ship's company. One September trip, at the time of the equinoxal gales I shall never forget. We were heading for Madeira with pupils from Staffordshire when we encountered Force 12 Hurricane Hilda blowing its way out in the Bay of Biscay. Devonia had no stabilisers and at the height of the storm the ship rolled 35 degrees each way constantly. Portholes smashed, furniture, usually anchored flew and passengers staggered around to find a safe place to settle. The school matron, Ena, an ex-Wren, was a tower of strength and with her team of assistants ministered to the miserable, seasick children and made sure they stayed in their bunks in their dormitories. As the hurricane raged, she was searching for a little lad who seemed to be missing. Nothing for it, but to go out onto the foredeck. There she found him wedged under one of the fixed wooden seats. Having winkled him out and brought him down to us, she returned to her cabin opposite mine. Later that day she showed me a postcard which inadvertently she had taken from this boy as she helped him off the deck. It was a card of the ship, - very white, with black and white funnel, in a blue, blue sea. He had written "Dear Mum, wish you were here. Instead of me".

That day I spent trying to balance against the roll of the ship whilst sewing up cuts and treating bruises. The steriliser in the dispensary sloshed hot water in all directions. Trays of sterilised instruments flew away as one worked. One little girl had a laceration from her upper lip to the base of her nose. With great difficulty I sutured it with a minute ophthalmic needle. I was delighted to receive a letter from her mother three months later telling me that she had no scarring.

Whilst this was happening an elderly cabin passenger presented with a fractured wrist. I knew the senior surgeon, despite the gold braid, would not be able to manage, so offered to set the fracture under anaesthetic. I gave the gas, then set the fracture, plastered it, and brought her round. As she went under the anaesthetic she sang "Nearer my God to thee". She didn't know how near she was, with my anaesthetic skills and a force 12 gale.

As she woke, she saw the senior surgeon standing by. "Doctor, you've saved my life" she said. With great modesty he replied, "It was nothing." How right he was!

So much to remember from this time at sea but some episodes stand out. We were to arrive in Leningrad in the summer of 1965 with a group of 10-14 year old pupils. A young boy presented at the surgery with symptoms which, following observations, I diagnosed as an acute appendicitis. The policy was not to operate on board but divert to the nearest port for medical care. To operate on board, the ship has to slow down, the itinerary has to be altered and visits ashore cancelled. General upheaval for everyone. We alerted Leningrad that transport to hospital was needed for this boy and an escort. Procedures for coming ashore in Russia could take hours and we were apprehensive for our patient. We docked at 6.00 a.m., and I was able to leave the ship with the boy by mid-morning. In an ambulance car with a university student interpreter we headed into the countryside outside the city. I had no idea where we were going or the plans made. I had no passport because these were collected and kept by the immigration officers. Eventually we drove into a wooded park to what looked like a large country house. The car was directed to park outside some huts in the grounds. We were taken into a small room with a low bed, a bench and a potty. Eventually the doctor, a large woman wearing a white headscarf and white uniform arrived and our interpreter spoke on our behalf. The doctor was doubting my diagnosis and, quite rightly, took a throat swab. Our lad choked at this, and tears welled up in his eyes. I remember telling him how brave he was, and that his example would be one the Russians would remember. He did stiff upper lip immediately. They agreed to take him to theatre. At this point the interpreter said she must go to lectures. Help! I was left, not knowing where I was, but I had promised the boy I would not leave him. I asked the interpreter to give me a note. It says I think "I am Dr Swallow. Please take me to my ship Devonia". Immediately I stuck it in my bra for safe keeping as a trolley came to transport the boy to theatre. The big white clad lady doctor indicated that I should leave. I said no, I had promised to stay with the boy until he had been to theatre. There was a lot of shouting, as our girl interpreter left. I told the lad to hold my hand and not let go until I said so. Great shrugging of shoulders, more shouting, and we went with the trolley out among the trees across the park into the main building where I saw him into theatre. I was shown into a waiting room, given tea and a doorstep of ham sandwich. I fed it to the birds on the window ledge.

To my surprise I was invited into theatre and grudgingly congratulated on my diagnosis as the all women team removed an appendix at bursting point. At the operation was a very tall handsome Somali medical student who spoke a little english. I showed him my note about returning to the ship. He was a life saver for he came with me by car back to the Devonia. Safe at last. What of our young student? He and his teacher were wonderfully cared for. They stayed free of charge in Leningrad, had a trip to Moscow, and then were flown home by Interflot at no expense. We were most impressed.

A less impressive episode involved a Scottish senior school on a trip to Lisbon. Unbeknown to any authority on board, their teacher had arranged a football match to be played on the Benfica ground. The ship heard of it at the last minute as the boys, early teenagers, left for the match. On their return we found they had been trounced playing Benfica's youth team and that one of our boys had been taken to hospital with a broken leg. None of this information came from the irresponsible schoolteacher. He did not seem to see the seriousness of the situation. The ship was due to sail in 24 hours time. We were not prepared to leave the boy behind in Lisbon. I was despatched to the hospital to see the boy. The impressive hospital façade got less impressive inside. Our patient, only just conscious, was on a low truckle bed, where an orderly was attempting to feed him with spaghetti. Big soccer player that he was, he cried when I said I'd be back that afternoon to take him to the ship's hospital. A conversation with the hospital staff indicated that he was not being discharged.

That afternoon I returned in a taxi with our nursing sister. We instructed the driver to be ready to drive away quickly. It is the only time I've done patient snatching. We found a wheelchair, went to the ward, put the boy in the chair and made a run for it. We made it back to the ship just a short time before we sailed. The teacher was told by the Ship's Headmaster, that his school would not be popular if they applied for a further cruise. We nursed the boy until we got back to Scotland where we transferred him to an orthopaedic unit.

As well as medical duties all officers were expected to be part of the team entertaining the independent adult passengers. Some of them became, what we called chronic cruisers, coming back time after time. Part of my role was to act as hostess at a table in the dining room. This meant welcoming and conversing with so many people during the course of a year. I would be one side of the round table for 10 and the nursing sister off duty opposite. It could get very tedious if we had a group of uninteresting, or non-conversational passengers. So we devised a merry wheeze to lighten our day. At the first dinner of the cruise, one of us would order the wine, and as we tasted it say, Happy Birthday sister or, next cruise Happy Birthday doctor, as we took turns to get things going. It worked well, especially being followed with drinks after dinner, or flowers at the first port of call. Things got difficult however with the chronic cruisers, many of whom would choose to sit at our table. One would say, "Oh, I've got you in my birthday book for September," and so on. We then had to dissemble and flee after dinner.

Off duty in Tangier

We also shared in entertainment for the pupils in the evenings when they had a choice of things to do. My singsongs seemed very popular, probably because they loved the deck officer who did it with me. No added accompaniment, just singing our hearts out and having fun. Between the officer and myself there was a lot of banter which the children enjoyed – "I say, I say, I say. Why are the sickbags double lined?" "I don't know, why are the sickbags double lined?" "To keep the flavour in!" Real schoolboy humour but they loved it. We also played fierce deck hockey matches against crew members and party leaders, as the teachers were called.

Fun fair nights and fancy dress parades were also popular.

For staff like myself the post was a wonderful way of seeing the world, learning tolerance of other cultures, and getting paid for it. Time off in port was time to see the sights.

The Little Mermaid, Copenhagen

Pyramids at Giza

The Kremlin, Moscow

St. Mark's Square, Venice

From Egypt's pyramids to the Winter Palace in Leningrad, the Belem Tower in Lisbon to the Jacaranda trees along the waterfront in Funchal. I have memories to last a lifetime. Always good companions to go ashore with and sometimes get into scrapes. I remember coming back to the ship with a large fish in Istanbul. It would make an Indian fish curry that evening. Frances, the nursing sister and I were being pestered, as always, by a local youth who was too forward with his hands. Our solution? Hailing a taxi, getting in one side and out the other on the busy road so losing our assailant after Frances had whacked him with the fish.

I also had my golf clubs on board and played golf in places as far apart as Bombay, Copenhagen and Funchal. On board one kept fit because one's only transport was walking on hard decks and companion ways. It was tempting to eat and drink too much free food and wine, but wisdom prevailed.

As ship's doctor I had to play a big part in any accident or emergency. Fortunately, these were only practice events but still taken very seriously. I would be in charge of stretcher bearers going to fires, simulated, in any part of the ship. One quickly learned one's way around from the engine room to the bridge and all stops in between. I also had to be ready to be in the crash boat which was launched for man overboard exercises.

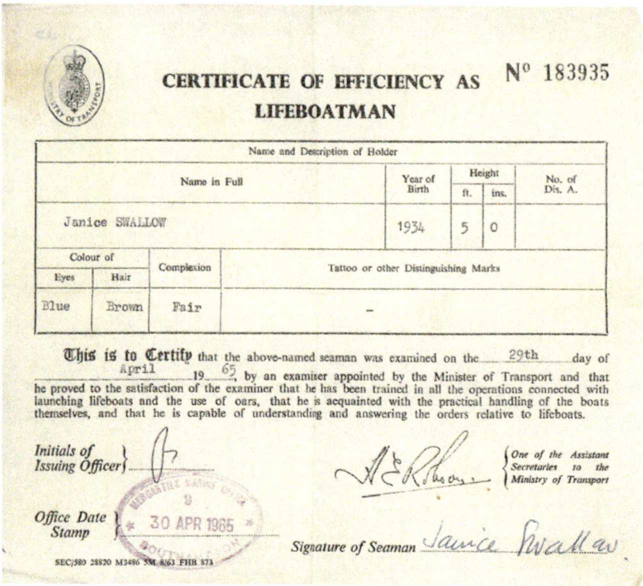

MINISTRY OF TRANSPORT

CERTIFICATE OF EFFICIENCY AS LIFEBOATMAN

N° 183935

Name and Description of Holder				
Name in Full	Year of Birth	Height ft.	Height ins.	No. of Dis. A.
Janice SWALLOW	1934	5	0	

Colour of Eyes	Colour of Hair	Complexion	Tattoo or other Distinguishing Marks
Blue	Brown	Fair	–

This is to Certify that the above-named seaman was examined on the 29th day of April 19 65, by an examiner appointed by the Minister of Transport and that he proved to the satisfaction of the examiner that he has been trained in all the operations connected with launching lifeboats and the use of oars, that he is acquainted with the practical handling of the boats themselves, and that he is capable of understanding and answering the orders relative to lifeboats.

Initials of Issuing Officer

One of the Assistant Secretaries to the Ministry of Transport

Office Date Stamp 30 APR 1965

Signature of Seaman Janice Swallow

SEC/580 28820 M3496 5M 8/63 FHB 873

I am a lifeboatman

The smallest firefighter training in Liverpool

During my time at sea, I gained both Board of Trade Lifeboat and Firefighting certificates. One lovely event made possible because the captain trusted me with lifeboats happened in Amsterdam. Two youngsters, boy and girl, on a junior cruise had been in the ship's hospital with chicken pox until the last port of call, Amsterdam. Still possibly infectious, they were not able to go ashore with their party. I asked the captain if I could take them into the canals in the small crash boat. To my amazement he allowed me to take a full size lifeboat with the help of an engineer officer at the engine casing and me at the helm. These were open boats about 25 ft in length. With captain's blessing, we put the two youngsters into the boat and lowered it down to water level. I, of course, was looking the part, in uniform and tricorn. A BI flag was on the engine casing. The children were so excited as I spread out a map of the canals whilst at the tiller. First stop, the customs post on entry to the city proper. The engineer went to their office beside the canal to explain our arrival. He was denied entry. Misery all round. I wondered what a bit of gold braid and feminine persuasion would do. I told the sad but true story of children saving up for the trip, doing paper rounds for a year to be able to see the sights and then the misfortune of confinement to the ship's sick bay. The customs officer was nearly brought to tears and gave us the all clear to explore Amsterdam. The map was like a street map, but for us, on water. Full ahead, turn right to the end of this canal, turn left, and so on. In a very pretty canal, lined with houseboats with check curtains and geraniums at the windows, we went under a bridge, ducked a little to go under the next bridge, and then I flattened myself at the helm to go under a third. No further could we go. Nothing for it, but to do a three point turn with a large lifeboat in a small canal at lunchtime in Amsterdam. Watched by office workers on lunch break I steered the boat first forward, then very slowly back getting closer and closer to the check curtain of the nearest houseboat. As I looked behind me, I saw a housewife rise up with the spaghetti she was eating dangling from her fork. I was in touching distance of her kitchen window. Then full ahead and round we went making our escape to the sound of applause from the canal-side. Heading back to the ship, feeling very chastened, we were shocked to be stopped again at the customs post. A fine? Imprisonment? Anything seemed possible. But out of the door came the officer armed with bunches of tulips for the children. He had been touched by my story and knew nothing of my faux pas. We didn't tell the captain.

Sovenier hunt with student from sick bay. Itea, Greece

Another contrasting story of pupils ashore involved a large contingent of American students whose leaders had chartered the ship to go to Egypt in August, although advised against that time of year by BI. In terrific heat we escorted these very self-confident teenagers to Cairo and the pyramids. That evening we had some itchy problems in the surgery. We found that many students had bought stuffed camels some 2 ft tall from roadside vendors. The camels were the culprits, bringing fleas on board. In the consulting room we opened up one leather camel to find it stuffed with bloody rags. The captain was informed and ordered all camels to be thrown overboard. What a sight. The trumpeter in the student band played the Last Post as the convoy of camels, feet up, bobbed behind us in the wake of the ship.

I was able to spend Christmas of that year 1964 at home with my family. Gifts were very special, having been bought on my travels. My niece and nephews loved any toys from abroad. Leather goods from Italy and Morocco made good presents for my parents, who still found my shipboard life bewildering coming from a generation where travel was a luxury. The plan for the Devonia for the coming year involved taking the Asian crew back to Bombay and then signing on a new crew. In January 1965 in Genoa we welcomed a small number of adult passengers for what was to be a six week trip to India and back. No school parties were on board and so the living was easy. A winter of sunshine travelling through the Suez Canal and Red Sea calling at Aden and Karachi. At Aden we took on board some families who had been to Mecca. Tiny babies with earrings and henna forehead markings who cannot have been more than a few months old. All looking sickly.

There was a drama when it was found that these passengers, mostly women, were cooking in the dormitories. A fire hazard of some magnitude. They disembarked at Karachi and the ship went on to Bombay. I was Senior Surgeon for this trip with an excellent colleague Jackie as Assistant Surgeon. We had one nursing sister, Gay, full of common sense and humour. We were sad to say goodbye to our personal stewards and hospital steward. They were to join the crew leaving to await the train to Calcutta. In the four days in Bombay, I said goodbye to dear Abdus Salaam as he proudly took a bicycle and sewing machine ashore. Precious items he had saved for and bought in Aden.

We kept them in the hold with the medical equipment until he left.

The new crew I was responsible for signing as fit for duty were a sad looking group. All very thin and looking old for their years. Anywhere else they would have been unfit for work, but I knew how vital it was for them to have a job. I reckoned, rightly, that fresh air, regular meals, a decent bed and a guaranteed job would improve their wellbeing dramatically, and so it proved. The deck crew were a special group. They all came from one village each year selected by their head man on board, the serang.

I said to Abdus as he left, "What will you be doing when you get home?" "I sit memsahib" he replied, and he meant it. No work was likely to come his way until he signed on again for BI in the future. In our four day stay we saw poverty I had never envisaged before. One of the most shocking sights was of young beggars with misshapen limbs deliberately deformed in order to earn their food to live on.

Having signed on the new emaciated crew we set sail for the return journey to Genoa. Our cabin passengers had enjoyed a sunny relaxed time and were planning their duty-free purchases in Aden on the way home. Sadly, illness in the new crew put paid to their trips ashore for the next three weeks. We had learned that there was an outbreak of smallpox in Calcutta at the time our new crew were leaving. So it was with some anxiety that we found three young men who had travelled together to Bombay presenting with rashes. Whilst we had seen chicken pox in our limited experience, we had not seen smallpox. We knew that smallpox distribution on the body is different from the lesser disease, but these young men did not really fit safely in the chickenpox category. What to do? The three of us debated this and resolved that to be safe we must isolate the patients and make sure all on board had up to date smallpox vaccination. This caused great consternation and some criticism of myself among the passengers, some of whom had to be vaccinated. We had a very busy time vaccinating all who had embarked in Bombay, for we did not trust the Indian certificates as we knew that water rather than vaccine had been used in the past. This had been told to us by our hospital stewards.

After four days our patients were improving, and we were happy to accept that chicken pox was the cause of the illness. This of course made us look foolish among the cabin passengers, but the captain assured us that we had done the right thing in keeping the ship safe from a virulent disease.

We had other things to worry about whilst this was going on. A crewman who had joined at Bombay, whilst he had no rash, had a very high swinging temperature, up to over 104°C and then coming to normal for a short time, before recurring. He looked very ill and complained of headache.

At 6 a.m. the hospital steward came to my cabin. "Memsahib, man in crew hospital not want breakfast." To which I replied, "He's a sick man and not hungry. Give him water only." "But Memsahib he goes "Chi, chi, chi" all the time and cannot speak." I realised he, Abdul Rahman, was fitting and that this was cerebral malaria. I was up at crew hospital like a shot to examine him again. With Jackie and Gay, we studied the books, looked at our dispensary, and planned for the care of our very sick patient, a gentle man who tried to cooperate in every way despite language difficulties. With steroids, antimalarials and analgesics we nursed Rahman, with one of us at his bedside 24 hours a day until the planned admission to hospital in Malta.

Malta at that time was a communist country with Prime Minister Dom Mintoff no friend of the UK. Our reception on the island was not good. Although we arrived at 8.00 a.m., we could not let passengers ashore until the ship was granted pratique – the certification that the ship is in good health. The port doctor, a large man, smoking a cheroot, strolled on board at 4.00 p.m. I immediately took him to see Rahman lying on his bed, bare chested and only wearing a lungi. As the doctor entered the sick man tried to say 'salaam'. The response of the despicable doctor was to lean over the patient letting his cigar ash fall on Rahman's bare chest. I so wanted this poor man to be admitted to hospital that I managed to keep my anger under control by walking out of the cabin for a second. It was agreed he should be admitted. We had already packed all Abdul Rahman's things and written necessary letters to the hospital. Nigh unto death Rahman was escorted in the ambulance by sister Gay to Valetta Hospital. His heart stopped on the journey. Gay revived him, but tearfully told us on return that she felt he would shortly die. But this happily is not the end of the story which takes us further into my time at sea and somewhat out of context with the journal. In

September 1965 I was instructed to leave the Devonia, then at Greenock to join the S.S. Nevasa, then in dry dock in Falmouth. The Nevasa was the last troop ship in the United Kingdom and had been commissioned by British India for its centenary year of 1956. It was unfortunate for the Company that the Ministry of Defence abandoned shipping troops around the world. Whilst they flew to zones of conflict, their equipment went in logistic ships, e.g., Sir Galahad, Sir Lancelot and Sir Bedivere. These were all manned by BI officers. The Nevasa, then out of commission was a white elephant for BI and was cocooned up the River Fal in Cornwall. It was brought down to the Falmouth dockyard in 1965 to refit as a school ship. Hence, my involvement, as I was to tackle the refitting of the medical department, much larger than that I left in Scotland.

On packing my trunk to leave I found Abdul Rahman's old slippers in the bottom of my wardrobe. I packed them in my trunk and drove to Falmouth, where on unpacking, they went back into my wardrobe. After two crew changes on the ship in the next two years, I was passing the galley one day when a crewman threw himself at my feet and said, "Memsahib, you saved my life." "Abdul Rahman, is it you?" As indeed it was. "And if you come to my cabin, I have your slippers." Why did I keep them? We shall never know – one of life's mysteries yet unsolved. But it was then a problem for me, for Rahman, plus slippers, returned to crew quarters where he told his story. The Indian crew all decided I had special powers, and from then on, I was accosted with requests for medical help for their families at home as well as for themselves. The Senior Surgeon at that time was not too pleased when Indian crew members consulting him, asked to see me. Very embarrassing.

Now back to my story of time in Devonia on return from India in late February 1965. From the heat of Bombay we returned to winter in Genoa where the ship had had a refit over Christmas 1964 before we sailed to India. In the few days we had before we sailed once more in the Mediterranean with schoolchildren on board, we had a few days to acclimatise. The Genoa representative from Mission to Seamen invited us to go skiing for a day, just two days before we sailed. The ship's officers took up the offer with delight. The first time having a day ashore for so long. We boarded a coach heading for Frabosa Soprana in the Maritime Alps. As we approached our destination high in the mountains our cheery host from the Mission said, "Hands up, how many have skied before." Not a hand went up. "Mamma Mia" he cried. "My advice? Don't be frightened and benda-ze-knees!" Our introduction to skiing therefore was rudimentary. Nursing sister Gay and I had taken the medical bag anticipating trouble. Unfortunately, I was the trouble. Watching people going up in a drag lift to the nursery slope I thought – I'll have a go at that. So, remembering "Don't be frightened and benda-ze-knees" I launched myself straight down the slope, not having had instruction otherwise. I whizzed down, eyes watering in the icy cold air. At the bottom someone said, "Jan, you're a good skier." Spoken far too soon, for on my next downhill whizz I caught my ski in some soft snow at the end of the run and collapsed in a very painful heap having twisted my left knee. The Italians watching went into full volume drama mode, trying to carry me feet first up a steep flight of steps to the rest room. I yelled for Gay with the medical bag. She arrived in the nick of time to shoo them away with a few expletives I hope they didn't understand. End of my ski experience for some time. The knee was very painful, and I suspected I had a tear in my medial ligament. With high drama I was stretchered off the mountain and with all my companions arrived back late that night on board. Whilst Gay and I had had Captain's permission to go, some had not asked for leave and were in big trouble because they were absent when ship inspection took place that morning. I knew I had to be able to work when we sailed in 36 hours' time. I was sent for x-ray and to see a consultant in Genoa. This entailed walking, in agony, up a long flight of stone steps to see a doctor who bound my knee with a viscopaste semi-plaster bandage. That night as the knee swelled the bandage became unbearable. I begged Gay to cut it off. Reluctantly she did so when I promised I would plaster my leg the next day. At 5.30 next morning, the hospital steward had a great surprise when he found me in the dispensary with my left leg propped up whilst I put it in a full length plaster cylinder. I knew this was the only way to protect it from the continual movement of the ship at sea. It did the job very well, and over the next six weeks the pain went, and the swelling went down. During that time, I was always on duty, and I took to the dance floor each night and also went ashore. One never to be forgotten night of the full moon I climbed up the Acropolis in Athens and wandered by moonlight around the Parthenon. Magical.

1965

A New Year a New Ship

SS Nevasa

Christmas 1965 was very much a contrast to the predecessor when I was at home in Luton. The cruise over the festive season for Devonia was advertised as visiting the birthplace of Jesus and singing carols in the Bethlehem fields then taking the tour of Old Jerusalem. Theory and practice differ.

I was informed at the beginning of the two-week trip that December that I was the only member of the ship's company who was to escort over two hundred school pupils, teachers and independent cabin passengers on the overland coach journey which would take us from Beirut in Lebanon through Syria and Jordan to Jerusalem on Christmas Eve. I learned that I would have a room in the Jerusalem Hilton that night. Because this was before the 6 Day War it was only permissible to go from Old Jerusalem into New Jerusalem which was to be our route back to the ship in Israeli waters at Haifa late on Christmas Day.

Six coaches and a spare left Beirut at crack of dawn on Christmas Eve to travel in convoy throughout the day to our destination in Israel. One employee of the head office of British India was the only company representative besides myself. He travelled comfortably in a car with an interpreter whilst I was in the last coach of students and teachers. He had only one point of contact with the other coaches in the form of a walkie-talkie, long before the days of immediate communication.

All went well until a coach broke down and I was turned out of my coach and instructed by my BI colleague that I was to be picked up by the military escort car which was following the convoy, some distance behind the passenger coaches. On the roadside in the Syrian desert I watched the last coach disappear into the distance. No-one in sight. No buildings in sight, but a lot of sand. No means of communication. After what seemed like hours, I saw a camouflaged army car approaching. It stopped and seemed to have instructions to pick me up. Inside were three armed soldiers. The driver, a sergeant, was very large and just about fitted behind the steering wheel. I greeted them with a cheery, "Hello," and a broad smile. It was only after the episode that I pondered on the danger I could have been in. The saving grace was my two-reel heavy Grundig tape recorder with which I was taping the whole trip. My companions were fascinated. I won them over by singing "The Sun Has Got His Hat On" and encouraged them to sing with me. They were delighted when I played back their efforts. It was sung many times as we drove onwards with the light fading and headlights made out our way. Thanks to the breakdown and delays, the escort car reached Jerusalem after midnight. No room at the Inn has a significance for me different from the usual image. My room at the Jerusalem Hilton had been sold to someone else. Where was I to go?

These splendid soldiers took me to the United Nations School where the women teachers and girls were staying overnight. I don't think any of the teachers, who were cross at the disturbance made to their slumbers ever knew of my adventure.

The day in Jerusalem was a full one. Due to our delay, there had been no carol singing in Bethlehem fields, but we did visit Jesus' birthplace and had a comprehensive tour of Old Jerusalem before we all had our passports checked as we left by the Mandelbaum Gate, watched again by Israeli armed guards.

One of the longest days I can recall for, on re-joining the Devonia at Haifa, I was expected to take part in the Christmas Gala Dinner and the revelry that followed.

It was in October 1966 that Nevasa made her maiden voyage as a school ship. She was popular with the education departments of most counties, and with the independent cabin passengers who enjoyed her facilities. The accommodation for the ship's company was also improved and I liked my cabin which was close at hand to the surgery on the hospital deck. The two nursing sisters had cabins beside mine. Involvement in all aspects of ship life was still enjoyable and the opportunity to visit so many very interesting places during employment was an especial attraction. To know that, within the year one could have the chance to stroll round Venice more than once was a joy. At that time it was a much more gentle city, not overrun by tourism. Copenhagen, Lisbon, Athens were all high on my list of special visits. In fact, this was the time I fell in love with Greece. That love has stayed with me into old age and become a treasured part of my life.

Entertaining cabin passengers was still expected of officers so unlike the cruise ships today, or, as I prefer to call them floating blocks of flats. I felt I had bitten off more than I could chew, when looking at the programme for Boxing Day on the Christmas cruise of 1966, I read that the entertainment involved bingo. In disgust I called the staff captain and pointed this out to him. "You can't play bingo on Boxing Night." "Well, what should you do?" "It's the time to have a party, a pantomime or concert." Reply, "If you want a bloody pantomime, you do it." Answer, "I bloody will."

In my cabin on Nevasa

This was ten days before Christmas. With so much going on I really could not see how we could put on such an entertainment with no professionals on board. However, I set to and wrote a whole panto in rhyming couplets, and, to pay back the staff captain's challenge, I made him a major player. He was tall, with reddish hair and not like a fairy, so he became 'Fairy Fortyinbras' in a tale of pirates and derring do at sea. One scene was to have Jolly Jack Tars with tankards, sitting around a barrel with a lot of yo ho ho and Jim lad planning dastardly deeds. But where could I find a barrel? All beer on board came in cans. Then the chief steward came up trumps. He remembered that in trooping days the ship had a traditional rum barrel for the regular crew issue. He went in search and came up from the hold where the barrel had been stored for years. It was perfect. An oak barrel, brass banded with 'The Queen. God Bless Her' in brass letters on the side. It, and the panto were the success of the season.

We were leaving the ship at Southampton after that cruise and were on leave whilst a refit took place for about 3-4 weeks. The senior representatives from head office arrived on board as we reached Southampton, awaiting dry docking. I sought out the Supplies Manager for cruise ships who had arrived from London and was enjoying a drink at the bar. I engaged him in friendly conversation, and said, "You know the Nevasa's rum barrel? As there is no call for it now, could I buy it?" He, a little in his cups, had no idea what I was describing and said, "My dear, you can have it, for being a good girl." Whoopee. How to get it off the ship which was teaming with customs officers looking for elicit goods? After some thought I wrapped the barrel in a Moroccan blanket and put it in my wardrobe. Two weeks into the refit, I drove down to the ship in Southampton dry dock, took the barrel from my wardrobe unaccosted and drove home. It is now one of my treasured possessions and a talking point with visitors.

In Spring 1967 the ship undertook a unique voyage across the Atlantic to Montreal, Canada. A Swiss company chartered the ship to travel with adult passengers only, from Le Havre to Montreal to visit Expo '67 held in that city. Language difficulties were eventually overcome as we took seven days to cross to

Canada, sighting distant icebergs. Before we entered the St Lawrence Seaway, we had taken into the ship's hospital an elderly Swiss man who had had a stroke. After discussion with the Captain and Head Office, we were advised that he was to be admitted to hospital ashore at our first port of call which was Quebec. Quebec at that time had just had a visit from the French President General de Gaulle, who had emphasised that Quebec was French territory. This gave us trouble, as there was antagonism to a British ship and no-one keen to speak english. When taking this man to hospital, the only thing they seemed bothered about was "Can he pay?" and sight of his insurance policy. However, we did leave him in hospital there and I'm afraid I know nothing of his fate thereafter.

Expo '67 in Montreal was well worth visiting with pavilions of so many countries. The Canadian, French and American were the largest and spectacular, but our British pavilion I think was more fun as we were able to laugh at ourselves. This was the year of the Mini, the Beatles and Mary Quant, and all featured prominently. There was a wonderful potted history lesson of the past centuries, from stone age to the present day illustrating two thousand years of development of a country.

I did not take to Montreal as a city, probably because we were only there for four days. One of those days was taken up going to New York for the day. Not many people have done that from our side of the pond. Again, a disappointment, as our guide told us of the tallest, the biggest, the most expensive etc., as our coach toured the city. We did however go to the musical 'Funny Girl' on

Broadway, before the tedious, cold coach journey back through the Adirondack Mountains to Montreal. Still, all in all, a three week trip worth remembering.

It was in 1967 that I was instructed to stand by the Uganda, which was in dry dock in Hamburg. The MV Uganda and MV Kenya were BI cargo liners. They had plied trade from the East Africa coast through the Suez Canal to England. When war closed the Canal, it was no longer possible for BI to carry out trading with these two ships. Like Nevasa previously the Uganda was to be converted to a school ship. The School at Sea had been such a success that there was need of another vessel. The conversion of a cargo liner was a much bigger challenge than a troop ship had been in '65. In Hamburg, the cargo holds were to be made into deck space for dormitories and other facilities for the schoolchildren. Classrooms and a swimming pool were two of the additions to be included. As with the Nevasa my duty was to set up the medical flat, and I spent over a month in Hamburg whilst the ship was made ready for its new life. Not ever having been designed for passengers only, it never felt as well-proportioned as its predecessors. The Staff Captain of the ship had sailed with her for some time previously and fortunately knew the ship's workings inside out. He was a consummate seaman and loved his job. I got to know John and his wife Jill very well over the time we sailed together, and so much so afterwards that I became godmother to their daughter and Jill was a witness at our marriage, John being at sea at that time.

In the course of the next year at sea on Uganda, I began

to tire of the routine and felt it was time to come ashore. The past four years had been rewarding, exciting, interesting and unusual. The fact that I had no family ties made it possible for me to value these years, when foot loose and fancy free. Unattached and in my mid-thirties I think I felt it was time to settle down. I was not quite sure what that would entail, but I knew it meant leaving my life at sea behind. I made so many friends and learned to be tolerant of other cultures in those years. And both of these assets have stayed with me through the years, I say with gratitude.

1968

I Come Ashore, Discover Bristol and a New Way of Life

Coming ashore with no future plans gave me time to consider my career. My family came back into the forefront of my way of life once more and adjustments had to be made. I returned to my parents home in Luton whilst I thought about what to do next. My brother Hugh was a partner in a local GP practice and suggested I might join them. This was put to the senior partner, a quite dour Scotsman. We met and talked, and although he was keen to have a woman in the practice, he dropped the bombshell by saying that I would not be expected to marry whilst working with them. I told him I had no plans for marriage but found that proviso quite unacceptable. I departed, to tell my brother that I would not be joining him.

I was not in a hurry to seek further employment and spent time visiting friends made at sea, and those from medical school days. Among the latter was Nancy Watts, a GP in Parkstone, near Poole in Dorset. She lived there with her mother, a relationship which put restrictions on Nancy's social life. She did however develop her talent as an artist, and on one visit I admired her picture of a trawler under construction at Seahouses in Northumberland. She wished to give it to me. I said, "No, I'll buy it, and one day I can say That's an early

Watts." Years later, having bought her picture for five pounds, Nancy in retirement was selling paintings from her exhibitions at several hundred pounds a time.

I also visited my god daughter and her parents John and Jill Young. I enjoyed their company and got to know them even better when I took up my next post. This was as a medical officer in a practice for Bristol University staff and students. I had decided that having enjoyed my time with young people at sea, I would continue to do so in this way. I quickly got to love Bristol, a lively city with an interesting history and civic pride. In my time there we were not made aware of the association with the slave trade, nor the wealth of the city made from tobacco. Now both have left a question mark over the city's prosperity.

I enjoyed finding my first real home, a flat, Melville Court in Hampton Road, where I had the top floor in a complex of three new flats. Furnishing it and settling in were new experiences and kept me busy. The practice comprised four members, Derek being senior partner. His number two partner was an interesting middle-aged lady, who was wedded to Bristol and knew everyone of note in the University. Although in her fifties she wiped the floor with me at squash, although she smoked like a chimney and would probably have collapsed running for a bus. She had some objectionable habits, one of which was to let her rough coated dachshund, Copper, use my consulting room carpet as a lavatory. Since she never took him out or exercised him it was understandable that he developed bad habits. The other partner was a younger married man who was my contemporary at

Bart's, where he had been an active member of the Christian Union. This was relevant to my role in the practice, since, not willing to sanction termination of a student's unwanted pregnancy himself, he then referred them to me, knowing that I was likely to do so. He also was loathe to prescribe oral contraceptives either. This in 1968, was the early days of the pill and counselling on contraception was part of our role. We were a mixed bunch as a practice, with Derek, the senior partner being very cautious to keep the University hierarchy satisfied with our performance.

We had a practice secretary Jen, who had been an assistant manager at a hotel in the Ceiriog Valley in North Wales, in a hamlet, Llanarmon Dyffryn Ceiriog. She spoke so warmly of her time there that I agreed to join her on a weekend visit to her old haunt. It became a weekend of some significance, for I met a friend of Jen's who has become a lifelong friend and part of my life to this day. "You must meet Liz Taylor" I was told, and immediately visualised star quality and a glamorous lady. Far from it.

This Liz Taylor was a local farmer who was an active member of the hunt and ran a livestock farm in the hills above the valley of the Ceiriog River, a tributary of the River Dee, south of Llangollen.

Elizabeth Taylor. Not that one - the sheep farmer

We planned to meet for dinner at the West Arms, Llanarmon on Saturday night. As we sat by the blazing log fire, whisky in hand, a call came to Jen from Elizabeth. She would be late because she had to get help pulling a cow out of a ditch. When this ruddy faced, stout unique individual eventually arrived with apologies, I liked her at once. Always laughter where Elizabeth was, challenging opinions and interesting conversation.

During that first meeting she described the farmhouse at her small farm Cefn Canol. Whilst she lived at the family home Bronydd in Glyn Ceiriog she used the farmhouse only at lambing time and let it during the year. On the strength of that information, we visited the farm next day and I agreed to take the house for two weeks in the summer of 1969.

This proved to be an eventful two weeks. My brother Hugh and wife Erica had by then four children under 10, Nick aged 8, Sarah 7, James 5 and Andrew 2. It was arranged that I would take the three elder children to Wales that summer. Great planning went into getting there. Their parents with Andrew brought the children to stay overnight at my Bristol flat, whilst they themselves stayed in an hotel nearby. An early start for Glyn Ceiriog next morning got the children settled quickly for the night. At 2 o'clock in the morning, I had a very distressed call from my mother in Luton. "Jan, I think Daddy is dying and I can't get hold of Hugh." She had forgotten our arrangements in her natural anxiety. I explained where Hugh was and said, "Have you called the doctor?" "Yes." "So, hold Daddy's hand and pray." I could not think of anything she could do, knowing her capabilities. Having called back as agreed ten minutes later, the doctor had arrived and lay Daddy on the floor to attempt resuscitation until the ambulance arrived. I have thought so much about this since. His own GP, not available, knowing that Daddy had had two previous heart attacks, would I feel have let nature take its course, but the one attending lived nearby and was a contemporary of mine at Bart's and possibly felt he had to act heroically. The outcome was that Daddy lived for two further weeks in the Luton and Dunstable hospital, with tubes to every orifice and an overwhelmed wife beside him day and night. Meanwhile Hugh and I resolved that I should take the three children to Wales, giving Erica and himself time to cope more easily at home.

We had a time at Cefn Canol full of fun and new experiences. Liz was exciting for the children to be with. She treated them like adults, and they responded by doing her bidding in all ways. They learned to be wary of farm implements whilst helping with hay making. We picnicked by waterfalls, played hide and seek around the farm, got to love the farm cat and Lizzie's dogs, Rip and Lady. It had been understood from the outset by the children that should Gramps become more ill, we would return home. This happened 10 days into the holiday. I told the children as they drank their hot chocolate at bedtime. Nick's response – "Well I suppose if Gramps didn't die, he might get measles and chickenpox and things." James aged 5 "It's not fair, who's going to teach me things now if Gramps isn't there?" Sarah (Twink) couldn't speak. She buried herself in the bedclothes and wept.

My father was a long suffering, intelligent schoolmaster, who at the time of his death was Vice Principal of Putteridge Bury Teacher Training College, now University. He had as related been a headmaster in Luton throughout the war and beyond. He had a heart attack at the age of 45, treated with rest for 3 months. No further attacks until in this year age 66, when he had another more severe attack in February. He was about to accept the plan to return to work in the autumn when his last heart attack occurred.

Poor Mummy, feeling so distressed and unable to help, sat at his bedside. When I arrived, I was upset to see my poor father propped up in bed with a drip up, and catheter tube by the bed. For what? Here was a man of great faith, not overly fearful of dying, and accepting his lot. He had smoked an enormous number of cigarettes in his 66 years. "Daddy, its Jan, I've come." Silently the tears rolled down his cheek.

The physician for the ward who knew both my brother and myself, was at that time on a ward round. We were in a side room with a small porthole window in the door. His face came to the window, and he moved on.

The experience of that morning at the L&D hospital I know was a great influence on my future career in medicine. There must be a better way to care for the dying I resolved. After a further 2 days Daddy died, leaving a wife who was ill prepared for widowhood. She had never even had a cheque book, could not drive a car and had always depended on the help of other people. This was a significant change to the lives of my brother, his wife and myself. Not so immediately for me, as I had to return to my job in Bristol, but my brother took on a role of head of the family. From then on, he was the decision maker. My mother began to rely on Hugh and Erica in so many ways. Being of a pessimistic nature she tended to worry over even small things, which was a trial for the family. There was little I could do to help but when, once a month, I had a weekend off I drove from Bristol to Luton to help Mummy, tending the large garden, which was getting overgrown. It was a relief when she moved to live nearer the family in a smaller house with a manageable garden in the nearby village of Streatley.

Whilst the late 1960s and early 1970s were a time of

sadness with the death of my father, whom I loved dearly and respected, despite teenage set-tos, it was also a decade when I made friendships which were to be lifelong.

One of these was with Miss Anne Jones. Anne and I first met when, as Assistant Matron at Bristol Royal Infirmary, she showed me around the nurses sickbay. One of the Student Health Service duties was care for the health of the Hospital staff in Bristol. I was doing my routine weekend visit to the sick bay when Anne was on call. I thought I had left my days at sea behind, but as she introduced me to a nurse in a bed in the sickbay, this patient cried, "I remember you. Last time I saw you, you were dancing on a table on the Nevasa!"

Anne was very Welsh, having been born in Tonypandy in the Rhondda valley in the very sad days of the '20s. She never forgot her upbringing in the poverty-stricken town with unemployment rife. Anne was not only a nurse but also a midwife and loved her nursing career. She was a staunch Methodist and had a flat in the house of another Methodist nurse, then retired, Maudie.

Anne and I hit it off from the start and enjoyed the same sense of humour. We spent spare time together, sharing meals and visiting the cinema. We also took picnics into the lovely countryside outside Bristol. So began a concerned friendship which lasted until Anne's death at the age of 90. Like Elizabeth Taylor, my farming friend, our lives came together from the start.

A most significant friendship was with members of staff of Clifton College Preparatory School, the junior part of

Clifton College, the well known Bristol public school. The pupils from Clifton Preparatory School were regular travellers on the School Ships. It was on board Nevasa that I first met Gwllym Isaac and Greville Rimbault, who came as masters with boys from the school. Gwll was a talented musician and before arrival at Clifton had been assistant organist at Canterbury Cathedral. Greville taught french and english and had been Assistant Headmaster on the Nevasa and Uganda. Our paths however had not crossed at sea. As I went down the gangway for the last time on August 6, 1968, and Greville joined the ship two weeks later. It was following this time at sea that he had recently come to Clifton Preparatory School.

The Captain of the Uganda, John Young as previously mentioned, lived with his wife Jill south of Bristol, and we spent many happy days together when he was on leave. It was John who was determined that I should meet the masters. He was in fact the matchmaker for Greville and myself. Whilst at Student Health I had taken some annual leave, acting as Assistant Ship's Surgeon once again on the school ships, specifically at the request of the organisers of the Prep School annual cruise at Easter time. They enjoyed my involvement socially, both with pupils, staff and cabin passengers. The prep schools produced one of the most amusing episodes of educational cruising worthy of a diversion in my memoir here.

The pupils on these trips at Easter time were always lively and inventive. No more so than the group who took the ship's headmaster's advice one year when he lectured about Morocco as the final port of call of the cruise. He advised them to barter with any currencies they had left with the traders they would find on the quayside in Tangier. It was not until the sailing music Hearts of Oak and A Life on the Ocean Wave was blaring from the loudspeakers as we eased away from the berth that we became aware of the disturbance on the shore. Numerous traders were running after the ship, shouting and shaking their fists.

Why? It was not until the school office was issuing board games that evening that we found that the Monopoly money had gone. Any currency had been taken literally by these bright young passengers. No doubt in later life they were bound for the Stock Exchange. But, poor British India had to settle our debts with the Moroccan traders at our next visit.

To continue: John and Jill came to dinner with me, and without my agreement, called Greville to join us after dinner. I was happily unattached, although was often finding myself paired off at drinks and dinner parties with rather boring single men in their late thirties. Assistant Bank Managers seemed to feature, in fact anyone introduced to me after one of my talks on life at sea which I gave to Rotary, Round Table organisations and the like. The BBC also became interested in my exploits and I talked on local radio and Woman's Hour.

I was guarded in my welcome to Greville but over the coming months as we saw more of each other, we found we enjoyed each other's company more and more. We played a lot of tennis, had cinema and theatre outings and got to know more of each other's history and background. Greville had had an unhappy divorce, which meant he saw very little of his 7 year old daughter Tessa and twins Harriet and Sophie, aged 4. They were in the care of the maternal grandparents, and whilst Greville had free visiting access, the custodians were most antagonistic and treated Greville unkindly. I think in retrospect Greville escaped to his job at sea soon after the divorce when emotions were raw. He obviously was cautious about any further relationship and I was equally wary of involvement.

But John Young and Gwil Isaac were keen matchmakers, as also was the headmaster of Clifton Prep School, Jim Hornby, who had become a good friend. He and his wife and large family had entertained me on many occasions once they knew I was in Bristol. Jim was an outstanding headmaster and one of the most friendly, welcoming people I have ever met. It was a great sadness that he died, far too young, of a brain tumour whilst still in harness at Clifton.

Bronydd, the home of my other lifelong friend, ElizabethTaylor, became my happiest port of call when I had a weekend's leave. I would drive to Glyn Ceirog in North Wales and delighted in time to spend in the Welsh countryside. The drive there was also special since it took me through the Wye Valley. Lizzie lived with her father who had been a widower for some years. He had been the manager of the Ceiriog Valley Company, quarrying slate in the local mines. The village had prospered through the mining of slate, but that was now a past industry. Captain Taylor, as he was known, had been part of a local shoot, and there was always well-hung game on the menu, produced by their housekeeper Margaret Conway and her husband Ken. Neither Lizzie nor I enjoyed the game but found Margaret's meals otherwise delicious. Lizzie's father was a keen collector of antique wine glasses, porcelain and clocks, which I found very interesting. He also had a wonderful wine cellar. He died soon after I got to know him and his daughter. It was one of Friday night's special treats for us to sample the vintage wines which Lizzie decided were going to waste. In fact, some were quite beyond drinking, but others were memorable.

Whilst having dinner together at the West Arms at Llanarmon one weekend I said to Lizzie, "I wouldn't mind having a cottage up here for my old age." My old age came more rapidly than I had anticipated, for next visit Lizzie said, "I've found a cottage for you." I emphasised again that this was an old age wish and no way could I find the money for such an outlay then as I was paying the mortgage on my Bristol flat from my modest salary at the Student Health Service. Persistent as always, Lizzie said, "Well at least have a look at it." So I visited the semi-detached three bedroom cottage Cor y Llwyn on a steep lane in the Glyn valley, just below Lizzie's home Bronydd, which had extensive wooded land around the house.

When I had climbed the steep steps up the garden path to the front door, I was met by the owner and numerous children. There seemed to be a child, including a baby in a pram, whichever way I looked. It was obvious why the house was for sale. It reminded me of the old woman who lived in a shoe. I can visualise so easily standing in the little bathroom with the owner when I asked what price he was expecting for the sale. In a melodious Welsh voice, he said, "I'm asking two thousand five hundred, but I'm open to offers." As I left with Lizzie, I said how much I liked the house, but there was no hope of me finding the wherewithal. I only had £700 saved which had been left to me by my paternal grandmother.

Back in Bristol, I put the matter out of my mind, but at my next Glyn visit, Lizzie was keen as ever that I should not let this offer slip. Again I emphasised that it was out· of the question. "Well, why don't I lend you the money, and you can pay it off bit by bit when you can afford it?" I could not believe what Lizzie was suggesting. But after much discussion and thoughtful agreement, the offer of two thousand three hundred pounds was made and accepted. I was the proud owner of a cottage in North Wales as well as my Bristol flat. We discussed the arrangement with a family solicitor friend of Lizzie's, Dudley Richards. He said, "You realise that this is the easiest way to lose a friendship?" We assured him that would not happen, and it never did. On reflection, I realise that we had no agreement in writing, just trusted each other. Cor y Llwyn became a special part of my life. A place to go to from the world of work. I met so many people there whom I loved. I had already met the two farmers, Walter and Albert Lloyd and their wives Julie and Ginny whilst at Cefn Canol. It was a joy to visit them in their farm Cefn Isa on the steep hillside above my cottage. They lived together in their farmhouse for all their lives. It is not often that two wives will share a house with their brother husbands. I took my niece and nephews to Glyn many times as children, and always took them to help milking in the old parlour at Cefn Isa. Nick was very keen on milking the cows and in fact carried his little radio from home to Glyn because he had read that cows gave more milk when milked to music. On one occasion Ginny was in tears of laughter quietly standing by Nick, as, with great concentration he milked a long-suffering beast. Ginny nodded for me to look where he was directing the milk as it squirted down Ginny's wellington boot.

So many happy times were given us by the Lloyds. Especially at hay making time when the children came home on the tractor with the haycart, ready to help stow the bales in the barn. Because I had only just managed to acquire the cottage I had to look out for second-hand furniture for it. This was fun. I took a lot of stuff from Bristol second-hand shops up to Glyn on the roof rack of my car, including beds and guttering over the course of that first year of ownership. I could not afford to employ craftsmen, so did as much DIY as I could. I repainted the house, much needed, outside and wallpapered and painted inside. A new lining went into the Rayburn stove and storage heaters to the bedrooms and sitting room. This was also my first chance to grow my own vegetables, with the assistance of muck from Lizzie's cows and horses brought down the steep hill to my back garden, where it was chucked over the hedge.

North Wales is a beautiful part of the country, and it was a chance to range widely over the hillsides in the

Berwyn Mountains or picnic above Llangollen, looking down on the River Dee bubbling along the valley below, and to the town bridge beyond from the escarpment called the Panorama.

Whilst seeing patients in Bristol, I met one whom almost by accident I took under my wing. Lyn, highly intelligent, was about to take finals in biochemistry. Her great anxiety was that wishing to do medicine, she had to get a first in her science degree to be taken on the medicine course. She needed to talk, and I gave her time to share her ill-founded worry of failure. It was well into my lunch time, and to give her space to continue I said she could come shopping with me whilst she continued her flow of worries. She carried my shopping basket as it was filled for that night's dinner party and coming back to my flat I offered her a coffee. I found then that she came from a Mormon family where no stimulants were permitted. We eventually settled for a hot chocolate. When I next went to Glyn, Lyn came with me. She lacked social skills and did not seem to have friends, but Lizzie, the straight talker, was sympathetic to her behaviour, and has over the years given Lyn hospitality on many occasions.

Whilst life in Glyn was progressing happily, so was my friendship with Greville. That summer we took a trip to Brittany and fell in love with its small coastal towns and hamlets and unusual rock formations. I can see how it fits in with Cornwall.

Greville proposed to me at Clifton Suspension Bridge, and as I cheerfully accepted, he gave me an engagement ring of sapphires and diamonds. We planned to get married just before Christmas. When I asked if I might have Friday December 15th leave, senior partner Derek said, rather testily, "Is it really necessary?" I explained about the marriage plans, and he agreed but added, "You must be back on Monday." The week of Christmas with many students away would not be busy but he could not be that generous.

Just married. December 15th, 1972

We had the quietest of weddings on December 15th, 1972, but joyful. Gwll Isaac and Lizzie were our witnesses at Bristol Registry Office, and Jill Young was also there representing herself and John, who was at sea. We returned to my 2nd floor flat after the brief ceremony. My dear friend and Health Service secretary, Jen, had left a bottle of champagne on my doorstep, which I found that morning when I went to collect the milk. This was to be drunk at home before we headed out for lunch. As Gwil popped the champagne cork, up at the 2nd floor flat's window came the window cleaner. I opened the window saying, "I know chimney sweeps bring good luck for newlyweds, but we are centrally heated. Will you join the toast?" Greatly surprised and a little precarious on the top of the ladder he agreed. We had a memorable, long lunch at Harvey's restaurant, where we were made most welcome.

We bade farewell to our guests and set off to the Wye Valley for our mini honeymoon. Back to work on Monday!

It was not long after our marriage that Greville returned to sea. He was offered Ship's Headmaster's post on the Uganda. Much as I was disappointed that our life together was to be disrupted so soon, I knew how much he had loved his experience at sea, so I encouraged his acceptance of the post. It also meant that our association with Clifton Preparatory School ended. I was still in contact with Gwll and with the Hornby family. I continued working for the University Health Service in Bristol. I have the glass goblet which was our wedding present from Senior Partner, Derek. Its engraving commemorates the return of Brunel's ship the SS Great Britain to Bristol for restoration on its recovery from the Falkland Islands. Its return after many years as a hulk of a coal carrier rotting away in the far British territory was made possible by the philanthropic anglophile, Jack Hayward. I watched it being brought up the Avon and, for the first and last time, going under Brunel's magnificent suspension bridge. Now it has been restored to its former glory as a passenger steam ship, and it is a great tourist attraction in Bristol dock.

I was back in my single way of life again and am glad I had so many varied interests to keep me occupied. I loved dressmaking and made many of my own clothes using couturier patterns – Givenchy, Dior – which I bought from the lovely old store Jolly's in Whiteladies Road. They had a wonderful selection of dress materials, so I was in my element choosing what to buy. I also made a lot of my niece and nephew's clothes too. I particularly remember dressing gowns for Nick and Twink, with rabbits to match, made from the remnants left over. I enjoyed complicated fine cross-stitch embroidery of bell pulls, and tablecloths too.

I continued my trips to North Wales where Greville joined me when on leave. We came to know the local countryside so well. Lizzie introduced us to Borth-y-Gest in the Llyn Peninsula. Such lovely sandy beaches with views across the estuary to Harlech Castle.

1975

'Man Proposes But God Disposes'

Because Greville had to pay maintenance for his three little girls, it was not our intention to have a family of our own. But, as Greville commented at the time, "Man proposes, and God disposes." So, when, despite our intentions I found myself pregnant, we had to rethink our future plans.

Relationship with the girls grandparents who had custody of the children was strained. Greville was blamed for the breakdown of the marriage after such a short time, but on reflection I realise that it was a precarious relationship from the outset. His wife was under 21 when they married, an only child with not much love shown to her by her wealthy mother and belligerent father. When I met them, on the rare occasions they would agree for us to take the girls out for the day, there was no warmth, no welcome, never invited into the house, and strict instructions for them to be back by 4 p.m. Not easy to get to know stepdaughters in such circumstances.

Things came to a head when Greville asked for them to come on holiday to Glyn in the summer holidays. We were told that this had made them so disturbed that they had had to see a child psychologist. I am not sure how I managed to contact the psychologist, but he agreed that he would meet us, with the girls, when we next took them out for the day. When we collected them at the door, Greville spoke of our arranged meeting with the psychologist. Grandfather, florid anyway, looked as if he might explode. "You have no right. How did you contact him?" A long tirade. Greville quietly explained that the arrangement had the blessing of the expert, who said it was important for him to meet us. We took the children to a play area for a picnic, and had a happy time together, though brief. Having observed the interaction between us, the psychologist concluded that he could not think of two people more fitting to be involved and give the girls a holiday, but added, "You know the trouble? You'll never win." The grandparents had bought their love with material things. They blamed us for their need to buy a Range Rover, a motorhome, a swimming pool, a yacht and cottage on the Hamble River, and would therefore not let go. The children's mother during this time had remarried and had a new family which eventually comprised twin boys and two other siblings, both girls. They had set up home in Wandsworth.

The psychologist, having predicted our wish to be involved would be rejected, advised us to step back and wait for the girls to seek us out when they were more mature. So this we did. But during this time Greville paid maintenance, and school fees for Tessa. We never saw a school report, or were given any information about their academic progress, try as we may. Not to be outdone, grandfather then, knowing Greville had married a doctor, applied for further maintenance. This incurred barrister's fees and a hearing at Southampton, which collapsed with our information that I was not expected to work much longer, as I was expecting a baby. Grandfather angrily turned to Greville and asked why he had not been informed. The judge, summing up dismissing the case, said that what I earned, and my profession were irrelevant to the case, and that the information about my condition was not relevant either.

I resigned from the Health Service and took maternity leave awaiting the baby's arrival. I did not have any formal antenatal care. The specialist I had used for gynae referrals in the Student Health Service practice saw me on just three occasions. All was progressing well, but in the last trimester of pregnancy my lively foetus was still head up and not inclined to go head down as is normal. Howard John, the consultant and I discussed plans for the birth. Having tried to turn the baby on two occasions it was concluded that a caesarean section was the safest procedure to be sure of an uncomplicated delivery. I remembered my midwifery exam questions. What are the indications for intervention in delivery? I answered yes to them all, only 5 foot tall, size 3 shoes, breach baby with extended legs and mother over 40 years old. It was agreed that I would be delivered by caesarean section on March 11th, 1975.

I was well looked after by Anne Jones and the Hornby family at this time whilst Greville was away at sea. Jim Hornby invited me to preach at the school service in Clifton College Chapel one Sunday. Afterwards I received a cheque with the comment 'it will buy a wheel for the pram.'

Greville was kept informed of these plans. It seems it did not occur to him that perhaps he should be around at the time of delivery and beyond. He apparently was expecting to come home at his usual date for leave 10 days later. When the Captain heard of this, he sent him home from Athens, arriving late in the evening on March 9th. I collected him from the station not long before midnight and soon after arrival he was dead to the world. Tired out from travelling, he fell into bed as soon as he could. At 2.00 a.m. my waters broke, and I sat on a towel on the floor trying to decide what to do next. Having known the plans for the birth I was ill equipped for a normal delivery. Sanitary towels would have helped, but I hadn't bought any yet. Then I remembered that when I was skiing, I had wrapped a towel round each ankle when my ski boots rubbed. I went to the hall cupboard, taking out golf clubs, tennis racquets, Hoover etc and there at the back – my ski boots. And hooray! A brown paper bag in each containing the much-needed articles. Relief. Padded up at last. But by this time, I knew I was in labour and must do something about it. Greville slept like a babe. At 6.30 a.m. I called Howard John and explained that tomorrow's caesar must be done today. "Jan, what time is it?" "Six thirty." "Right, call the hospital and say I'm doing a caesar at 8.30 a.m. and will you get the duty anaesthetist?"

Talk about a do-it-yourself kit. I woke a confused husband and eventually arrived at Bristol Maternity Hospital, very much unexpected. Anyway, all's well that ends well, and Jenny Hallett Rimbault was delivered at 9.30 a.m. weighing 6 lb 14 oz.

I was unused to being on the receiving end of medical

care and found postnatal time in hospital stressful. So much so, that I said to Howard John when visiting, "This is the only place I know, apart from prison, where they take your clothes and you are kept until told you can go home." Whereupon Howard replied, "Oh Jan, go home." So I did. No follow up care was arranged, and this is where Anne Jones came into her element. She had been a strong support for me whilst I awaited Jenny's arrival, but now for her to be holding a newborn baby and knowing what was needed, made Anne delighted to help. Before Jenny was born, Anne and I visited Mothercare. I as a 40+ expectant mum and Anne, 60+, a maiden lady, we were uncertain what to buy. We eventually followed a lady who looked as if she were about to give birth in the store, and roughly bought what she had in her basket. No disposable nappies, just towelling squares and muslin liners in 1975. The first few months of a baby's life I found very unrewarding. In at one end and out at the other seemed to be all the little one had to offer, but it is soon apparent that recognition between baby and mother is taking place and that indescribable bonding takes place.

Greville was not in any way a 'hands on' father.

In fact, he was back to sea after two weeks and I was the equivalent of a single mum. In a second floor flat on my own, it was not easy. Carrying everything up and down stairs seemed to take ages. Jenny was not easy to feed and cried a lot, which was stressful.

Greville with 10-day-old Jenny

I had many sleepless nights in those first three months, and this is when Anne became heaven sent. She would call to find out what kind of night I had had. "I'll be round" she would say, and duly collected Jenny plus nappy stuff, bottle and feed and take the little one in her little carrycot pram off to her flat, whilst I put my head down and slept with enormous relief. Anne was also a good cook, and when I went to collect Jenny there was always a delicious meal for me. I cannot think how I would have managed without her help. My family was miles away in Bedfordshire, and my mother would not have been able to help, even if she had offered. Anne became a rent-a-granny and stayed that way for me for the rest of her life.

I think Greville did eventually realise that whilst he was having a high old social life on board, I was on my own. It was one of the reasons that he sought a further prep school post and came ashore. He was appointed Head of French at the Beacon School in Chesham, Bucks from the autumn term of 1975. That summer we had to make plans for our future as a family. It was resolved that the flat in Bristol be sold and Jenny and I would live in the Glyn Ceiriog cottage until we could find a house in Chesham. This duly happened, but it proved more difficult to find a house we could afford, and so resulted in Jenny and my stay in North Wales being longer than expected. Meanwhile Greville was given accommodation at the school. I can remember how much I longed for Greville to be at home with me again and how very disappointed I was that in the summer holidays from school, instead of coming home to be with Jenny and myself, he chose to do an English as a Foreign Language course at Norwich for nearly all the holiday time.

Whilst the memory of loneliness is uppermost in that first eighteen months of Jenny's life I came to really appreciate the friendships I had. Lizzie was always a cheerful companion, with her dogs, her horses and her farm. Anne often came to stay with me, and we found much to share together. The Lloyd family were close neighbours and always helpful. Jenny's first birthday was not spectacular. Ginny Lloyd came to tea on her way up from shopping in the village, and we lit a candle on a tiny cake!

It was in this year too that I got to know Jack Williams, the GP from Llangollen, who was responsible for patient care in Glyn. I had done an occasional Saturday morning surgery for him when I came up for the weekend from Bristol. But when he realised I was more permanently in the village he was delighted. He knew I could do with the money too. When he called and started a conversation, "Look gal!" I knew what he wanted. Two occasions were memorable and fun for me. The first was when he went off to a wedding leaving me to do morning surgery one Saturday.

During the session Lizzie rang to say she thought 'Percy' had broken his leg. Percy was a pet lamb now growing large and greedy. He ate all flowers in Lizzie's garden at the farm, and hence he was named after the local gardening TV celebrity, Percy Thrower. Duly after the surgery I went to Cefn Canol where I found that indeed Percy had jumped off the garden wall and broken a back leg. Usually, he would have been dispatched with such an injury, but Percy was a bit of a favourite with everyone. So, I plastered the leg, and off hopped Percy seemingly managing very well.

On return next day after the wedding, Jack called. "How did it go gal?" "Oh, quite straight forward surgery and one visit." "What was the visit?" "Oh, just a fractured leg." "Who was it?" "Percy Thrower." "Bloody hell gal, what did you do?" "I just set the fracture." By this time, I thought 'got yer Jack! I had given him quite a scare.

The second event – happened when a call came to the surgery. "Lulu's bad." Lulu was a rather pathetic lady who lived alone in a derelict terrace of cottages on Church Hill – a 1:4 lane out of the village. Jack Williams was very good to her and also shared a whisky with her on his way back home from evening surgery.

I said I would visit that morning. When I reached the door of the cottage, as I went in a rat ran out. Undaunted, I called into the dark interior, "Lulu?" "I'm here, I'm bad." This was the North Walean description of most illness. Having explained who I was, I tried to get a relevant story. Not easy. It did seem that Lulu, for some reason, had fallen downstairs and was complaining of a painful bottom. Having eventually managed to get her up the stairs with great groans, I examined Lulu on her bed. "Lulu, I think I know what's the matter." "What is it doctor, what is it?" she asked. "Lulu, you have put both legs down one leg of your knickers." For this I had trained for seven years!

So, Jenny and I were resident in Glyn until she was eighteen months old. Why was our daughter called Jenny? It was because I felt so in tune with the Leigh Hunt poem, 'Jenny Kissed Me.'

Jenny kissed me when we met,
Jumping from the chair she sat in,
Time, you thief, who love to get
Sweets into your list, put that in!
Say I'm weary, say I'm sad,
Say that health and wealth have missed me,
Say I'm growing old, but add,
Jenny kissed me.

Leigh Hunt 1784-1859

She was a very easy little girl, taking her first steps soon after her first birthday. She set off walking with Ginny, on a visit we made to Bodnant Gardens on the North Wales coast that spring. Such a beautiful place with the rhododendrons in full bloom, as also the laburnum archway and the pieris forrestii. Walking on hillsides from day one would make Jenny an agile walker from then on. She was also keen to talk and had, even at that early age, an excellent attention span.

This became more apparent when we were united as a family once more in Treachers Close, Chesham. An unattractive terrace house in poor condition, which was all we could afford in this town at the end of the Metropolitan line. Many residents earned London rate salaries, hence the house prices. Every day when Greville set off for school, Jenny would head for the tin of Smartie tops. We had discovered that if you bought enough tubes of Smarties you could collect an alphabet. One letter was found in the top of each tube all in varied colours. With a wipe clean board, she would clamber up onto a kitchen stool at the work top and, eyes closed, find a top and identify a letter. A circle was drawn round the letter until we made a string of balloons from our tops on the white board. She soon knew all her letters and not much later began to make easy words from our balloons. The most simple early learning device possible, but once she fell in love with books and reading, she was well away.

I hated our time in Chesham, which I found a most unfriendly town. Greville had a number of friends and colleagues at the Beacon School, but I was desperately lonely. Eventually I took the car trip over to my brother and family. My mother lived just down the road from Hugh and Erica in the village of Streatley, just north of Luton. Mummy had Jenny for a morning whilst I did a session in my brother's practice. The one I had declined to join previously. It gave me an opportunity to see some of the family, if only briefly, and a chance to help my mother too. My brother had been very helpful to us in our Chesham house, putting some shelves and cupboards in our little kitchen. I felt that the whole time we spent in Chesham was a time of DIY and work on the house and garden.

It was a respite from Chesham to be able to escape in school holidays to our North Wales cottage and be among the friendly folk there. Jenny enjoyed her little bedroom there with the spotted flycatcher nesting in the air brick by her window, and the tree creeper performing up the trunk of the fir tree close by. She was a fun little girl, and it was about this time that, when she was helping me get dressed after a bath that she handed me my bra, saying, "Here are your hump covers

Mummy." Lovely.

On another occasion when we were holding a little party for our Glyn neighbours, Jenny was in charge of a plate of cocktail sausages. She was doing very well, for a three year old when she said, putting down the plate, "Just a minute. I've got to do a burp in my bottom." Happy memories.

1978

School Days for Both of Us

It was Greville's intention whilst at the Beacon School to apply for a Prep School Headship.

Greville the school master

So it was that we found ourselves at Moyles Court School in the New Forest just outside Ringwood. We were there for interview for the post of headmaster of the school, starting in the spring term of 1978. The school was housed in a wonderful 16th century old mansion, which had been the home of Dame Alice

Lisle. She was famous for having hidden two Royalists at the time of the Civil War. She was tried by Judge Jeffries and condemned to death. Being an old, widowed lady and arthritic, the judge agreed that she would not be required to kneel for beheading and was hung instead. When at interview, Greville asked about the finances of the school, he was told by the Chairman of Governors, a solicitor, "Like most schools of this sort at present, we break even." We had liked what we saw. We were shown a new block built about 5 years earlier with science room below and dormitories above. We noted that it was not in use but were assured that numbers for the coming year were healthy. The school had an efficient maiden lady matron Collie, who had a very nice house outside the school's extensive grounds, which she shared with her sister.

We had a charming two bedroomed house in the grounds, beside an old granary, which stood on staddle stones and was most unusual and of historical interest. When we met the staff, we realised that they were mostly wealthy, middle-aged women who were not particularly committed to teaching, but it was a way of earning some pin money. They arrived in large cars just at start of school day and left promptly at three. The rest of the time the responsibility for the small number of boarders aged between 6 and 13 fell upon Greville and myself and Collie, with variable help from her assistant.

Within a few weeks Greville realised that the calibre of the staff was not what he was used to, and said to me, exasperated, "You know what would help? I'd sack the lot of them and get in teachers we know." It was when reading the minutes of the previous governors meetings before Greville's first meeting with them in that spring term, that he discovered he had not been told the truth about the school's financial situation or the projected pupil numbers for the next year. At that meeting he told the governors that he had been misled. The new science block had a massive mortgage, and he pointed out that if he committed his whole working days to the school, he doubted whether that mortgage would be repaid.

Soon after the meeting, one of the governors, John Bradfield, Headmaster of Walhampton Prep School at Lymington came to see Greville. He apologised, saying he should have spoken up at the interview, and made clear the situation of the school. He knew we had not been told the truth about finances or projected numbers for the coming year. Greville said he would continue in the post but be aware that things were precarious. The pupils at the school were of mixed ability but few whom one might call bright. The local parents choosing Moyles Court I always felt did not wish to be in the state system, possibly liking the smaller classes, but also the idea of a pretty uniform, the school's beautiful situation and fee paying appealed to them. We would have said the calibre of the teaching was not up to state standards in some departments. The boarding boys and girls came from complex backgrounds and from service families. They were few in number but had delightful surroundings in which to grow up. The school grounds were a joy. There was an adequate swimming pool, and the countryside of the New Forest was outside the school gates. Having taken up the post at the start of the second term of a school year, for five terms we tried to raise standards and improve finances. Alas, Greville decided in the summer term of 1979 that the school was not financially viable, and spoke with his deputy, a single lady, and then with the governors about his decision that the school, should close. They understood his reasoning and agreed. But local parents wished to put money into the school to keep it going, however unpredictable its future. At a parents meeting Greville explained the thinking on closure and the agreement of the governors. At this point the deputy head did a complete about turn, jumping up and saying, "We must fight to keep the school open" – and more besides. And so it came about that she became headmistress, took over our house and Greville, Jenny and I were left to find home and work. I had just started doing a session a week at Christchurch Hospital and I hoped to continue this. It was a morning in an orthopaedic clinic, but I needed to get back to my medical work in whatever aspect. One session a week was available and I could organise my home commitments to fit in.

It was a difficult time for us, not knowing what our future might be. It was made more difficult for me when the deputy head, quite quickly, was at my door asking what carpets and curtains I would be leaving. I just said, "We'll be taking the lot."

John Bradfield came over from his school, at Lymington. He was concerned for our situation and his part in it. He was full of apology to us. He said, "We've made a mess of our small number of boarding girls at Walhampton and I like how you've looked after boarders here." He suggested we took over the Clock House, which was for girls 8-13 years. Greville would teach french in the junior school plus english and games.

We had no option. It gave us accommodation in a flat alongside the girls dormitories and employment for Greville. I explained that I came from the state background and had not had experience of boarding school but was willing to give it a go. I also emphasised that as a doctor, my continued medical work would come first. John said he understood this and just hoped I might do the job until he retired in four years' time. I agreed to this. So that summer of 1979 we were moving house again. In her brief life so far, Jenny was moving to her fifth home.

Walhampton Prep School had a good reputation and was a feeder school for Winchester, Canford, Bryanston and Marlborough Public Schools, among others. My role was pastoral care for the 13 boarding girls. Their accommodation was in the delightful part of the school called the Clock House, where, as well as a dormitory for twelve, there were charming smaller two-bedded rooms. Walhampton House had a long history and had been the home of Admiral Sir Harry Burrard in the 19th century and in the 20th century was owned by the St Cyres family. In 90 acres of grounds were lakes for sailing, an area for a riding school as well as the usual cricket and rugger pitches, plus a swimming pool and tennis courts. Girls were a new introduction into a school which had been developed post war as a boys school by John Bradfield (JB) and his partner Peter Lawford. John had married the school art mistress,

Jackie, some years previously and she had overseen the introduction of girls to the school. She admitted, with no children of her own, that the girls were an unknown quantity to her. As John had described to us, they were a bit of a mess. They had been treated as pseudo-boys and tried to behave as such. They were rude and unpleasant to care for at first, but I eventually taught them how to achieve what they wanted with pleasant demeanour and good manners. I had had no experience of prep or boarding education, and on many occasions I felt sorry for them. The reasons for boarding were varied, but for some it was from families overseas or from divorced parents. I had a mixed role, sometimes matronly, sometimes motherly. I heard stories from these boarders which would have surprised their parents.

We started with just 13 girls, but we must have done something right, for numbers increased each year, and by the time of my resignation after 4 years there were 45 boarding girls. For the role of housemother I was paid a salary of £600. We also had a flat, rent free, attached to the large dormitory which was directly behind a door to our kitchen. It was not easy accommodation on the first floor of the Clock House overlooking a courtyard in which the pupils spent playtime. I got the girls up and ready for school daily and also had to supervise their rest time after lunch and finally oversee bathing, hair washing and bedtime. This meant being available from 7.00 a.m. to 10.00 p.m. to cover these times. I had an assistant who did the more menial tasks such as laundry daily, and supervising bed linen changes. I did not find pleasure in some of this work, but I knew I was supporting Greville in the school. He helped in a small way in the Clock House, but it was very much a feminine domain.

Meanwhile, Jenny was moving from a local playgroup to Lymington Infants School. We had no plans for her to be privately educated, although that had been the choice for her father, having been to Wellington College, like so many sons of army families. From there Greville had studied at Queens College, Cambridge. I went from Junior School to High School in the state system. It is interesting to realise that my admission as a non fee paying pupil in 1945 was the first year of free State Education for Luton High School for Girls, having passed the first 11 plus, whilst Greville moved from Prep School in Devon to his Public School.

I continued my sessions at the orthopaedic clinic at Christchurch Hospital. Again, not a job of choice but necessity as I was paid so poorly for my role at the school.

1978

The Beginning of a New Career

'God moves in a mysterious way.'

All things in the end work for good I believe, and so it was with my association with Christchurch hospital. It was at this time that I learned that my Aunt Wyn's husband, Leslie had had surgery for a carcinoma of the bowel. He had been given a colostomy. Knowing how fastidious this childless couple were, I could not envisage them coping with a colostomy. I called Auntie Wyn and in the course of the conversation I asked how they were managing changing the colostomy bags and so on. A greatly relieved Wyn replied, "Oh Jan, it's so good to talk to someone about such things. All my friends are very good and call, but talk about the garden and such, and not what I'm worried about." I told Wyn I would call her again in a day or two to give some support.

As I put the phone down it rang. "This is Dr Ronnie Fisher, from the Macmillan Unit at Christchurch. I wonder if you would come and work with me in the Unit?"

A call, out of the blue, but it was to be a most important call in my career, indeed in my life.

I replied that I didn't know, with respect, who Ronnie Fisher was, or what the Macmillan Unit was. Ronnie explained that the Unit was the first NHS terminal care unit, funded by the state, but built by the Cancer Relief

Macmillan Fund. Dr Fisher, an anaesthetist consultant, had been a tower of strength and enthusiasm in getting this Unit up and running in 1975.

As soon as he had finished explaining the role of the unit, I interrupted with, "Yes, I'll come." "Steady on," he replied, "it may not suit you." "I know it will be alright, I'll come." And so, my next 18 years in palliative medicine began.

I don't know if there is such a thing as a calling or an answer to prayer, but from Wyn's phone call to Ronnie Fisher's it seemed to me that I was being directed. It made me immediately recall the time of Daddy's death and my feeling that there was a better way to care for those in the last days of life. Now I had the opportunity to contribute to that better way.

I started sessions at the Macmillan Unit right away and liked what I saw and was ready to learn all the principles of care for the dying which were being introduced via the CRMF, as Cancer Relief Macmillan Fund was called.

For those in the last days of life, time is so valuable, and those involved in their care must appreciate this. No rushing from patient to patient, with not enough regard for what it must be like to be in bed, not by it. Time to be with the patient, time to help them to express their feelings and anxieties. Time to listen, rather than talk. Time to reassure and come along side someone who has a life behind them but not before them. Medication for symptom control was very carefully monitored on a day to day or even hour to hour basis as everyone is an individual and response to pain is unique to each one.

This meant that the Unit's nurses had to be specialists in pain control and in all the symptoms experienced by those suffering from terminal illness. In general hospital and general practice the use of opiates, such as morphine, or diamorphine, were viewed with great caution at that time, and indeed, prescribed sometimes in ill advised dosage. The Macmillan Service and the start of the Hospice Movement by Dame Cicely Saunders played a valuable part in teaching the use of medicines in palliative care. It was good to be part of this in its early days, and to realise now how far we have come in care of the dying.

In the Macmillan Unit I became aware of the need for teamwork. It was vital that each nurse or doctor knew their patients and their needs thoroughly and was able to hand over the information to the next team when going off duty. The teams were good, and I especially enjoyed working with my doctor colleagues, first under Dr Fisher, and on his retirement with his successor, Dr Fiona Randall, an intense, clever young redhead, who had come from St Christopher's Hospice, where she had worked with Cicely Saunders. She admitted that she was surprised to become a consultant in her twenties, and she had much to learn in the way of social skills needed to lead a team. Old enough to be her mother, I eventually drew her attention to this, but with moderate effect. Clinically however, she was very astute, and I learnt a lot from her. She achieved much in her clinical career and was highly thought of in the upper echelons of palliative medicine.

The Unit introduced me to the role of home care

nursing. A team of four nurses, who had all studied the specialty in a course on care for the dying known as the '931', were on daytime call 7 days a week to give telephone advice or home visiting to any of the patients on the Unit's books. Everyone referred to us by their GPs or local hospital was seen on a personal visit by our consultant, and a plan of care offered from then on. I would take on this role when the consultant had annual leave. I was known as a Clinical Assistant, and later as an Associate Specialist in Palliative Care. I made sure when accepting a patient into our care that they knew we would always be there for them. So many times, they would have been referred from one consultant or another with that dire phrase "there's nothing more we can do" ringing in their ears.

I would assure them that there will always be something more we can do, even if it's just a warm hug or a comforting word.

The Macmillan Unit had a few individual rooms but mainly small six bed wards. I felt privacy was important for families sharing in these last few days together, and not just the privacy afforded by a curtain round the bed. This was a concern I would take on with me into my future career.

Besides the In-Patient and Home Care Service, the Day Centre at the Macmillan Unit proved a great success. Many with life threatening illness can become isolated at home and anxious and depressed by what is happening to them. With transport provided, the Day Centre allowed them to leave their homes and come out for the day to a place where they could be understood and welcomed. A variety of activities was always on hand in the attractive setting of the Day Centre, with its garden, complete with fountain, fishpond and aviary. Many visitors were happy just to sit and relax with the small amount of energy they had left, but some would learn new skills, art, pottery and so on, with the assistance of volunteer helpers.

Whilst I was becoming more and more involved with my palliative care work, I was also still overseeing the Clock House at Walhampton School with Greville. The days were very full, starting with getting the girls up ready for breakfast and the school day. I would take Jenny to school in Lymington, before heading off for a morning session at Christchurch. On my return I would have to be in the Clock House after school lunch when the girls returned to the dormitories before afternoon games period. Soon it was time for me to do essential shopping and collect Jenny from school. This was vital time for me to share with her before preparing supper, and then into the dormitories again until all the girls were settled for the night and lights out. Often it didn't stop there as home sickness or minor illness had me back among the girls, whatever the hour of day or night.

I have always felt Jenny, although never expressed, resented the attention I gave to these privileged girls, whilst she was often needing to be left alone, Greville having duties in the school at unsocial hours also. I always tried to be with Jenny for some story time, but it was not unusual for me to return to our flat to find her fast asleep with the light on and a book beside her head on the pillow. Naturally, she did not understand the necessity for me to do this job, to give Greville a role at the school, and for us as a family, a roof over our head.

The school emphasised its Christian ethos, and indeed boys and girls were prepared for confirmation by the local vicar. How much they understood of the significance of what he taught them I did wonder from time to time. After one of these sessions as the girls got ready for bed, I asked, "Why confirmation?" To which the only reply was, "So we can get married in church." Sunday morning chapel was compulsory for pupils and duty staff alike. I could sometimes plead on call for Christchurch. We went to the chapel in the beautiful old music room of Walhampton House. The headmaster and his deputy were very committed Christians, and services were quite formal. The school choir took a significant part in the services.

Jenny was not keen on the morning service, and although she was at a Church of England Infants School, was not taken with hymn singing and prayers. She could surprise me from time to time. One Saturday morning I was showing prospective parents round the Clock House with the Headmaster. Jenny was trailing along behind me, aged 6, when the mother turned to her and said, "And do you go to this school?" To which Jenny immediately and vehemently replied, "NO WAY!" My heart missed a beat – was this a dismissible offence? Did John Bradfield think we were speaking ill of the school within the family? I could imagine the parents' conversation in the car as they left the school. "Lovely school, wonderful grounds but, that little girl must know something!" We weren't dismissed. They would never have got anyone as replacement for £600 per annum. The salary was due to change however, only with the arrival of a further blow to Rimbault plans.

Greville and I had talked together about the future, as I had agreed to undertake house mother duties for just four years, knowing that after that time John Bradfield would be retiring. This was the spoken agreement I had made with him that day at Moyles Court. I had no written contract. Greville was teaching, mainly french in the lower school, and undertaking other responsibilities within the school.

We felt it was time to look for a house in Lymington so that Greville could continue as an out-master and I could concentrate solely on my work at the Macmillan Unit. We found a house we liked and could afford, with a mortgage. Building Society and Surveyors were instructed, and we were looking forward to our plans going ahead. Then the spanner in the works. We agreed that I should tell John Bradfield our plans because the mortgage would depend on our salaries.

So, at my usual report daily to the headmaster I told him of our plan, reminding him that I said I would do the job only until he retired. He did not have to look up contracts or ponder his answer. Without any hesitation he replied, "Just remember Jan, if you go, Greville goes too." My world collapsed. I left at once, speechless.

We looked at Greville's signed contract and to our dismay read "to fulfil this role the applicant must live in the Clock House." John Bradfield knew what he was doing from the outset but did not draw our attention to this clause in the contract at the time of signing.

I am slow to anger, but I was angry. The next daily visit to the Head, the anger was expressed. "John Bradfield, I have realised that your Christianity is confined to short trousers and knee socks and I want no part of it." Again, I felt dismissal was about to take place. Not a bit of it. My salary was raised to £1,000 and nothing more was said. We discussed it among ourselves and resolved to stick it out until John retired. And so we did.

I felt it was important that the girls in my care should know something of the other aspect of my work. I talked to them on many subjects and explained to them a little of my role at the Macmillan Unit. They were keen to be involved. With John Bradfield's permission I took some of the girls to the Day Centre at the Unit. First, they did a Sunday Morning service with the Unit's chaplain, a dear retired Methodist minister, Maurice. Later we devised our own 'Favourite Things' programme, which was a great success. I encouraged all the girls to take part by either reading or singing a favourite song or poem, or, if feeling unsure of their talent, bringing a 'favourite thing' with them. So, rabbits and guineapigs were included, and paintings and pottery. Of course, the Sound of Music was our signature tune. The patients loved it.

Approaching death can be very hard, but I took great comfort that we were getting things right from remarks of patients and their families. One maiden lady stands out for me. She had been for many years housekeeper to the local catholic priest and had no immediate family. As I entered her room to admit her, she said, "Come in dear, I do believe you've been sent to see me across the bridge." This thought has stayed with me ever since and given me much to think about. She certainly had a strong faith in an afterlife, and her description of death as a bridge I found a helpful one when discussing the subject. A bridge is never built into a desert or a swamp, but into a place one wishes to get to. A bridge is a connecting link between two different places. A bridge is there because we wish to get to the other side which may be unknown to us, but a good place to be.

It was whilst I was pondering on my own faith whilst attending the services at Walhampton School that I began to think about the Quakers, the Religious Society of Friends. Because they do not evangelise it was difficult to find out about them, and at the local Christian bookshop I got a very prompt response to my enquiry. A negative response too.

I have described how, from time to time my life has been 'lead' with solutions to my queries and problems which were not of my choosing. This again was one of them.

From medical school days I had known Ted Cantrell, who qualified at Bart's about the same time as myself. All of us scattered on qualifying to our first house jobs at various hospitals.

When I joined the Casualty Department at the Luton and Dunstable Hospital, I found Ted was there on a medical ward. We had played tennis together at Bart's, and Ted, like me, was a hockey player. We spent six months working together at the L&D. I went my way and did not know what Ted did next. Years went by for me at sea and at Student Health. Then, when I was walking down the steep hill to the Royal Infirmary in Bristol, up the road came Ted. "Ted, what are you doing here?" "I work here." "What are you doing here?" "I work here." I invited Ted and his wife Beth, who had been a Bart's nurse, to come to supper. Not to be. Ted and Beth were leaving within the week to work abroad in Uganda. Ships that pass in the night. We went our separate ways again. Over ten years later Greville and I were walking in the grounds of Walhampton School after the storms of 1987. Many trees had been blown down and logs were on offer to the public. 'Fill your boot with logs, free.' "If I didn't know Ted Cantrell was in Uganda I would have said he was filling his car boot with logs" I commented. I went closer to the car to make sure. "Ted! What are you doing here?" "We live here. What are you doing here?" "We live here." Again, the invitation to meet up, and this time it was possible, for Ted and Beth lived close to the school. Ted was a senior lecturer in rehabilitation and consultant rheumatologist at Salisbury and Southampton Hospitals, whilst Beth, who had diverted from nursing to academia, was teaching at La Sainte Union College in Southampton.

God moves in a mysterious way. I realised that yet again I was being directed. Ted and Beth were Quakers, and Beth put a starter pack of Meet the Quakers through my letter box. 1987 was my year of first attending the local Quaker Meeting. The start of a way of life which I have found both helpful and rewarding ever since.

The simplicity and sincerity of the Quaker service when, in silence, we wait upon God was in marked contrast to the school's morning services. In Quaker worship anyone may contribute with spoken word, but the gathered silence in fact speaks loudest of all and to all. Some years later I committed myself to membership of the Religious Society of Friends, and I have found my involvement has strengthened my life. I have particularly found their small handbook Advices and Queries both a challenge and a solution to problems with which I might be wrestling.

Quakers conduct both weddings and funerals for members of the Society, and with my association with the Macmillan Unit I was asked to take on the responsibility for conducting funerals for the Lymington Meeting. I had previously only done a funeral service for a patient at the Unit. I had spent quite a time with her over the short time she had left, and after one conversation, she asked if I would conduct her funeral, which was to be a cremation service. It was impossible to refuse, and indeed I told her it would be a privilege to be involved.

From that time on I was to undertake that privilege for so many families. It was mainly with Friends, as the Society is known, but also I was approached by bereaved relatives who did not wish for a formal Christian service. I always told those seeking me out that my background and faith were Christian in origin, but that I did not conform to any particular denomination except the Quakers.

1983

Farewell to Walhampton

I ponder on the division of the Christian faith into various denominations with its roots in history. In this country, the Church's separation from Rome was to satisfy the wishes of Henry VIII to marry Anne Boleyn, with resultant dissolution of the monasteries and establishment of the Church of England. Across the continents of Europe and the Americas we see how man's power has altered Christ's message. I find this intrusion of man's power is not to my liking. I have therefore given denominational worship a cautious approach.

My time at Walhampton was coming to an end with the retirement of John Bradfield. Fortunately, he had not advised his successor, Andrew Robinson, of Greville's contract with its clause of residency. I took advantage of this as soon as the new Head and his wife Rachel were in post. Inviting them to dinner before the start of the autumn term 1983 gave me the opportunity to inform them that I would be leaving at the end of the academic year, and Greville would be an out-master. We had found a brand new house that we could afford in the middle of a terrace of three in the small village of Pilley, about a mile from the school on the edge of the New Forest. We planned to move during the summer holidays and had put our cottage in North Wales on the market. It sold very quickly to our next door neighbour.

We hired a van and moved everything down to our new home in Pilley.

I continued my work at the Macmillan Unit at Christchurch Hospital. I was taking on more responsibility within the Unit, and enjoyed doing locums for Fiona, our consultant, when she took leave. I was pleased to be working in the all women team. The other two assistant doctors, Elizabeth and Mary were a delight, knew their stuff and were excellent colleagues. Elizabeth, who was about my age had had a number of years working as a gynaecologist in Africa. Always calm, always reliable, a devout Christian from a medical missionary family. I admired her so much. Mary was a great foil, quite different in lifestyle, but yet again, a joy to work with and good at her job. She did however have a tendency to become pregnant on a regular basis. In fact, she managed to care for six children as well as part time sessions at the hospice. Her husband, Nick, was a local GP. We loved to hear the exploits of the family which were often hilarious. Mary was always willing to tell stories against herself and her children which had us in stitches.

And so, in August 1984 we set up home in Pilley, and, at time of writing have lived in 2 Trowbridge Cottages for 37 years, as I do today.

Trowbridge Cottages, Pilley

Jenny had been enrolled in the local infants school in Lymington soon after we became House Parents to the girls at Walhampton. I know she was pleased to leave the Clock House and for us to be together in Pilley as a family, with no responsibility for other people's children anymore. I always remember the date our house in Pilley was built, for the builder had included, high up over the front door, a black brick which was inscribed with the date of the birth of Prince William. Sadly, it is too high up to read unaided.

It was some time after Jenny had left the Infants School that I learned a heart-warming story about her from her former teacher. She was in some ways a typical only child of older parents. She was reticent to take part in group activities and would, if allowed, stay close to the duty teacher for example, at breaktime, avoiding the rough and tumble of the playground. The story was about the children's replies to their teacher's enquiry about what they wanted from Santa for Christmas. The Barbie doll, the Scalextric were much in vogue, and were the number one present of choice. Until teacher came to Jenny. "Now Jenny, what do you want?" After a bit of thought apparently, she replied, "I don't want anything, but I do need a new battery for my torch!" This has almost been a problem for me from that time onwards, for she really does not receive gifts with enthusiasm, leaving one feeling a failure when trying to please her. Unused gifts thirty years later can still be found tucked away in a chest of drawers. But I do not consider that response as a fault, and to this day she still illustrates that it is 'more blessed to give than to receive.' Jenny was our greatest gift and was such a joy to care for and love.

Jenny and Greville on a forest walk

She was bright academically. I really didn't teach her to read. At three years of age she quickly learnt to make words and then put them together. Her great love of books has stayed with her from an early age, when she chose a paperback classic at King's bookshop in Lymington weekly, and remained throughout her school and university days, her time in Russia and in Paris, until today, when with two children to read to, she stimulates their love of books too. Jenny progressed through school and university with success, and her life story is another journal in itself. Her love of language was stimulated by Greville's love of words and teaching french. Anne Jones, our rent a granny, also awoke her curiosity for Russia after Anne had toured there. Jenny then began to read any russian literature. Her Christmas present, aged 13, was a copy of War and Peace. I was sceptical that she would devour such a weighty tome at that age, but she certainly did, and from then on sought out Russian authors. I had bought a cheap paperback copy for the Christmas present thinking the book would soon be discarded. Not so. Her study of languages took her to Oxford, a degree in Russian and history, and afterwards a career in french translation, mostly of complex legal documents.

With Jenny in Paris

Nine years of enjoying the delights of living in Paris, was followed by return to London, when in 2009 she and her French boyfriend Richard decided to become an item and started their life together. Richard, a chef, could find work in any place and Jenny continued as a legal translator then at offices in Canary Wharf.

Meanwhile Greville and I were continuing our careers in teaching and medicine whilst settling into life at Pilley and being able to plan holidays at home and abroad, without having the responsibility for my cottage in Wales, which had meant spending my six weeks holiday a year from the Mac Unit visiting Glyn Ceiriog.

In the 80s and 90s we spent Christmas with my family at Streatley. During the Christmas of 1986 it was sad to see how unwell Mummy was. She ate little and rested up on a chaise longue in the dining room whilst we had lunch. Before leaving, I asked Hugh to make sure she was seen at the hospital. The result of this was a diagnosis of carcinoma of the pancreas. A surgical opinion was offered but, with my agreement, Hugh said he would take Mummy home, and tell her the diagnosis there. "I knew something was wrong" she said. "Hugh, do me in." And again, on the phone she asked me to 'do her in.' I went to Streatley and it was clear she had made up her mind that it was time to die, we having told her that as doctors we could not do as she wished. Did she want us both struck off? Erica and Hugh were very caring and nursed her at their home. She ate and drank nothing, set her mind on dying. And managed it, with as little distress as she could in a week. A very determined lady, she managed her own demise at 84. Her life had been hard in so many ways. No wonder she showed little love for me and was jealous of any success I might have. She loved her grandchildren, and latterly lived through them. I hope we gave her some happiness.

1991

Our Annus Horribilis

1991 was our annus horribilis and has become memorable for so many sad reasons. Greville's aunt Nan, was isolated from us and from her sister Joan my mother in law and her husband Geoffrey living in Surrey, because she had spent so many years living in Paignton, Devon. She was devoted to her little dog, her sole companion. No family, few friends and having an anxiety complex which made her lifestyle very lonely. After some diplomacy both with Nan and with Greville, I managed to bring Nan to live in a small care home on the sea front at Barton on Sea. Close to us, but sadly, not close enough to her sister for her to feel willing to visit. Joan was quite a tender flower cared for by a devoted husband. Nan loved her new life and was happy with her view of the Needles on the Isle of Wight. Time spent knitting, solving crosswords and, oh yes, I had found her accommodation allowing her to smoke. Greville's visits were a new pleasure to look forward to. Jenny and I also saw so much more of her.

It was at this time that the Walhampton School headmaster had indicated that owing to a decreased number of pupils, they were enquiring if any of the teaching staff was looking for early retirement as they were having to make plans for the future finances at the school. I am not certain whether Greville gave any indication that he was interested but events took over.

Meanwhile, in April 1991, Nan had a mild heart attack as described to me by her GP. I visited early next morning. Nan was sitting up in bed, breakfast tray beside her, Woman's Weekly on her lap, specs on the end of her nose, dead. Whilst it was a shock to me, it was also a shock to the home's staff who had taken her breakfast an hour ago. I had to break the unexpected news to Greville, who was predictably quietly upset. Not a man to show emotion easily, he retired into his carapace and busied himself with the practicalities of Nan's death.

June 1991 brought the next trauma, when Greville was told by the headmaster that he was to be made redundant. Not the term however used by the school, but nonetheless true. At the end of term address to parents, they were told that Greville Rimbault had taken early retirement. A shock to him and to me. The financial implications gradually sinking in. A small pension from his teaching career and my meagre salary for part time palliative care were limiting.

We needed to plan for the future, with Jenny, and our mortgage, in mind.

It was not long to wait until the next blow struck. In August Greville's mother, who was in her mid eighties, was taken into the cottage hospital and died within a very short time. An undignified death, publicly, for a very private person. It was clear to me that Greville's relationship with his parents had always been distant. At times of death in the family one takes stock of what has gone before. I reflected on the little I had learned of the relationship of this only son of a very social couple, who in the 30s had an army life in India, which did not include child rearing. Greville was born in Ranikhet in 1935, where there was summer accommodation for the British Army officers and their wives. Polo, pig sticking, and cricket seemed to fill the photos in the Rimbault album.

Nan came out to be with Joan in India when Greville was born and was devoted to this very pretty baby. Joan continued her social round. Evidence of this comes from the story Joan told of the time when she was hosting a dinner party one evening, when a guest enquired after Greville, then under a year old. It was only then that Joan remembered that she had left him some hours earlier down the garden in his pram.

The family returned to England when Greville was 2 years old. Geoffrey, as a distinguished soldier was serving in Palestine as the tempo towards war increased. He was a handsome man and courteous at all times. He won the military cross for his bravery in Palestine and would later win the DSO for courage under fire in Italy in the Second World War.

In the war Greville and Joan joined Nan in Paignton. Greville went to boarding school at 6 years old and remained away from home and parents from that time on, first at school, then university and then teaching in prep schools. Joan and Geoffrey showed little live emotion and so Greville inherited this from them. He could never be said to 'let his hair down.'

Thus the summer of 1991 was taken up with the two deaths and redundancy for poor old Greville. I supported him as best I could, but he was not easy to get close to at this time.

But this was not all the sadness for him in that year. After Joan's death Geoffrey sold up their Surrey apartment and moved to Devon. I have always found the speed and secrecy of the move puzzling. I think Greville did also but spoke very little of it. It appears that Geoffrey, who was a governor of St Paul's Girls School in London, had provided financial assistance via the Mercers Livery Company to the son of a young parent who was widowed. I do not know how involved with her Geoffrey was, but it seemed clear at Joan's death that the move to Devon to live with this widow had been planned beforehand. We were in touch by phone, but it was after he had settled in and was comfortably homed in his own apartment in the country house that we planned to travel down to visit, taking a hotel place nearby. Alas, this was not to be. A phone call told us that Geoffrey had been found dead in bed, having died in his sleep, about two months after Joan's death. Another trauma for Greville in this year of sadness. Another family funeral to be followed some time later by a splendid memorial service in the chapel of Mercers Hall in the City. Geoffrey had been a livery man for many years and a former Master of the No 1 Livery Company, the Mercers. Greville was also a Mercer and sat on several of their committees in his retirement. Incidentally, I too am a livery man of the Worshipful Society of Apothecaries. The memorial service showed how much respected and admired Geoffrey had been as so many representatives of facets of his life were present. Many from his regiment, the Loyals, of which he had been Colonel, distinguished cricketers, Geoffrey had been President of Surrey Cricket Club at the Oval, various sportsmen, as he had held the post of Head of the Army Sports Board for several years. A very special day of remembrance, but I wished Geoffrey had been there to see how much he was admired. I often felt such a father was a hard act to follow, and that Greville was over-awed by his father's success.

As 1991 was a year of many sadnesses, so the following year seemed to bring the silver lining to that year of cloud. The death of Greville's parents helped our financial situation, and we took advice from financial advisors on future plans. Greville meanwhile had taken a post at Beaulieu, the local Stately Home of Lord Montagu. Besides the renowned motor museum, the Abbey at Beaulieu was also part of Lord Montagu's entertainment complex. Here, Greville, dressed as a monk, acted as a guide in the domu and taught visiting school parties how to use a quill pen with simple calligraphy lessons. He made a good monk, although hair loss did not constitute a tonsure. It was later that year that an opportunity arose for him to return to what he loved most, namely, life at sea. He started lecturing on ports of call for P&O cruise ships. Living near Southampton, it was an ideal post. He would board such mighty floating hotels as Canberra or Oriana at the busy passenger terminal and be at sea for 2 to 3 weeks at a time. I had no love of these great liners which were ugly. New ships were launched as cruising became so successful. I did suffer one Christmas cruise when Greville was port lecturer on Oriana. Twenty-one days, with over two thousand people I did not know, travelling to Iberia and Madeira. The main focus on board seemed to be eating and drinking, and entertainment which I would not choose; bingo, quizzes, stage shows, dances. I felt like a fish out of water. Greville was always busy and I was always lonely. Not for me.

1988-1996

Oakhaven

I write now, of one of the most significant opportunities to come to me in what is left of my life. In 1988 a local GP, Dr James Soper, contacted me asking if I was willing to meet with one of his patients who had in mind to build a hospice. Her name, Mrs Phoebe Coates. Her husband had died the previous year and apparently, they had spoken together of the idea of building a hospice, in the grounds of their house in Lower Pennington Lane, Lymington. I agreed to meet Phoebe, little thinking that the conversation we had that day would be a life changer for me.

For all the time that I had worked at the Macmillan Unit, Christchurch, I had felt so sad for patients coming from Lymington and New Milton who often saw little of their loved ones because transport was so difficult. Phoebe's suggestion of a local hospice was to me a perfect gift. She was a quietly spoken, gentle lady with a core of steel, as I was to discover over the next few years. At that first meeting she asked about my professional history, "Do you think Lymington needs a hospice?" "Why do you ask?" I replied. She then said, "You know about these things, and if you'll do it, I will give you a quarter of a million pounds and my croquet lawn to build it on." This to me was an answer to prayer. However, I felt I must act with caution. I knew nothing of Phoebe and her background. I replied, "It's not if we think Lymington needs a hospice, but rather we need the opinions of the local doctors from whom patients will be referred." I offered to sound out the local GPs and report back in three weeks' time. In the interim I shared the news with Greville and Jenny, knowing it would take me away from home quite a lot if I was to undertake the work.

The general feeling from the GPs was a positive one, although a few did emphasise that they liked looking after their dying patients. I assured them that they would not be excluded from care if the hospice was also involved.

Three weeks later I gave Phoebe the news that we had doctors approval locally if we went ahead, but I pointed out that she should save her money if the local NHS Authority, based at Southampton, had in mind to build a hospice themselves in our area. Although I knew that there was little chance of this happening, I felt it necessary to let the local medical authority know what we intended. It was important to get their approval if nothing else.

I worked very hard putting together a paper giving evidence of need and how we could answer it in a feasibility study for the Area Health Authority. I then went to meet their chief executive and the representative from the nearest hospice which provided for Southampton area, the Countess Mountbatten. Having been quizzed for over an hour, their conclusion was that they liked what we were doing but could not help as they had no funds available. This was what I had anticipated and so when telling Phoebe the outcome of my visit, I agreed with her that this meant that we must go it alone and start a charitable trust. This we did, forming a committee of trustees who were to oversee all aspects of finance relating to the building, equipping and legal business for the hospice.

From this time on, Phoebe became a large part of my life. Most days, when I left work at Christchurch, I would visit her to discuss each move towards attaining our goal of a hospice in the grounds of Pennington Chase. I was keen that we should not be too ambitious but would cut our cloth according to our purse. We chose to offer for planning permission a five bed inpatient unit and a day centre, in a building suitable for the garden setting. We met frequently with our architect, Simon Nunn to discuss the project, taking advice on choice of builders. Whilst this was going on Phoebe and I thought of a name and a logo for the hospice.

Often we came to the same conclusion for a subject, after pondering independently. I said to Phoebe that I thought haven should be in the name, since a haven was a safe place to come to out of a storm. Phoebe thought the large oak tree which was at the side of the plot on which we were to build, should be included. Together we said Oakhaven, and so it became, with no other consideration. There were many times when things seemed God given and this was one of them. Even more so when around this same time I said, 'I suppose we have to have a logo" and Phoebe went to her desk and produced the die of the symbolic oak tree with nine leaves and five acorns, which has become so familiar to everyone associated with Oakhaven until the time of writing. It is as I write, in peril of being done away with. God given, it did seem to be that day when Phoebe produced it. She explained that it was in her possession being the symbol over the stall of John's sponsored chorister in St Bride's Church in Fleet Street, the journalists church. The Coates family was associated with printing in many ways, providing inks for newspaper print for example.

So in a trice we had a name and a logo. But that was the easy task. Planning permission was another matter. It was turned down by the local planning committee. One suggested Phoebe was trying to build a bungalow in her garden. Other adverse comments gave the indication that this committee were not in touch with what we had in mind. How to get permission on appeal? I knew we must be proactive. Phoebe and I went public. In a letter to the local paper I explained what we were aiming to do. Offering to the town, a facility for care of the dying, unique to the area and free to all in need. In rejecting our submission, I told the readers that it was like the town having its best Christmas present and not unwrapping it.

At the same time, we set up a stall outside the Parish Church where Phoebe worshipped, and where the Vicar, Rev Michael Joint was a keen supporter, having cared for his late wife until her death from cancer. The stall was the focal point for signing the petition for reconsideration of the decision on appeal. The appeal signing took place on the three Saturday market times, up to the day of the committee's convening to reconsider their verdict.

The result of my letter with its phone number was that I was called by numerous people in support of our enterprise. I made sure each member of the planning committee received any protest letter. The decision was overturned, and we were free to start building. Freemantle of Milford was the chosen builder and we soon realised how proud they were to undertake the work. They worked late into the day, and cleared up, regularly, so that the garden in which they were building was disturbed as little as possible.

Before work started the plot was blessed. Michael Joint, with Phoebe and I and some members of the Trustee Committee walked the boundary of the plot and as we did so, we recited Psalm 23, The Lord is my Shepherd and Psalm 121, I will lift up mine eyes. From that time on I would describe Oakhaven as measuring 121 by 23.

Work started in March 1990 and remarkably, our first Day Centre visitor was welcomed on November 14th, 1990. This was thanks to the co-operation of many, and the good weather in the summer that year.

Whilst I was housemother at Walhampton School, I had met Joy Toomey who was school nurse. A bright, cheerful pretty girl, who not long after our meeting married a housemaster, John, and became Joy Elphinstone. In conversation one day she asked me about my work in palliative care at Christchurch. "That's something I would like to do" she commented. It was a long time later that a vacancy for a staff nurse occurred at the Unit. I mentioned it to Joy and spoke for her with our consultant. Joy was appointed at interview, and so began working alongside me at Christchurch. I liked what I saw of her demeanour on the ward and how she worked in a team. So in 1989 I talked to her of the plans for Oakhaven, and my need to find the right team leader for the nursing team. I knew Joy would fit that role well, but by then, she had a young family. Apparently, her son Jonathan was enthusiastic for his mother to be Nurse in Charge at the Hospice. She agreed to my proposal that we should work together, planning and preparing for the opening of the hospice. One of the requirements I made for any nurse to work at Oakhaven was that they should have undertaken specialist palliative care training. This training course was done, in house, at the Macmillan Unit, and was free to nurses working in the Unit. Unfortunately, when Joy applied to take the course before taking up her post at Lymington, the consultant said she would not be accepted unless she paid the fee herself. There was an element of concern here since Joy and I were starting the new hospice together. Joy could not afford to pay for the course, and I could not appoint her without this qualification. To the rescue, paying the fee, came Joy's sister-in-law and her husband. It was a very kind gesture. It was done in memory of the baby they lost when very young.

Joy left the Macmillan Unit after her training later on in 1989, and from then on, she and I set to planning and ordering every item needed for the hospice, from carpets and curtains to all medical equipment essential to be in place before we could open our doors to the public, both for patients and for interested parties, of whom there were many. We shared all our thoughts on the way forward with Phoebe. She indicated early on that she trusted our judgement and would not interfere with the running of the hospice. I was also answerable to the Trust members for my actions and was required to meet with them regularly. Their expertise in palliative care was questionable, but they had the best interests of the hospice at heart, and that was important. Their main responsibility was financial, and that was certainly where their interest focused, since as a charitable trust they had to demonstrate that the enterprise was viable.

Much has been written elsewhere about the hospice, but I will record things personal to me. I met so many interesting people during my time as medical director, and one or two whom I would not wish to meet again. The challenges of each day were many and varied. My small team of medical and ancillary workers, many as volunteers, was the best. Their loyalty and willingness to help was second to none. An example is Cherry, who because of profound deafness had to give up teaching. She offered her help and was an asset as an archivist as years passed. She was an amazing lip-reader, having done it from childhood. Many had no idea of her deafness, although her intense watching of the speaker and her tone of voice gave it away. At the time of writing, over thirty years later, she is still involved regularly. Volunteers have made it possible to run the hospice economically as salaries increase year on year. After my retirement in 1996, I have been aware of the increasing appointment of paid staff, replacing many whom in earlier times worked for the love of the hospice. I was upset by a conversation with a senior nurse in an administrative role, who visited whilst I sat by Phoebe Coates in her dying days in her hospice. She said she did not see her work in Oakhaven as a vocation, but just another job. Fortunately, such attitudes still seem to be rare and the pride early employees felt to be part of the Oakhaven team is still there, although disturbed by bureaucracy as seems to be evident elsewhere.

Oakhaven's first staff photo
The Inpatient nurses, December 1991

Joy held her team together with a light touch, offering kindness and humour with her nursing skills. I loved working with her. I knew there was a problem to solve on arrival for the day, if she brought in what came to be known as 'emergency tea'. It seemed to work as a problem solver. We shared so many moments of sadness, hopefulness and occasionally drama together but also so much laughter.

Being in an affluent part of the country on the south coast, we did not experience the financial hardship of some other areas. Fundraising was rewarding and necessary. Often the source of funds came from legacies from grateful families having experienced the hospice's expertise.

One particular patient springs to mind for he arrived on an auspicious day in the early years. A call from a GP requesting an urgent bed came on May 7th, 1992. On this day, the Duchess of Kent was arriving by helicopter to formally open the hospice, which had then been functioning for eighteen months.

Formal opening of Oakhaven Hospice, May 7th 1992.
The Duchess of Kent with Phoebe Coates

I was told that the patient was nigh unto death with an aggressive bowel cancer. His doctor reckoned his life in days. The most pressing social problem for him was that his two children, one a consultant paediatrician in Johannesburg and the other a teacher, also in South Africa, were due to fly back home in 48 hours, leaving their 85-year-old mother to cope alone. With this information I agreed to admission, making the family aware of the situation that day at the hospice.

So, half an hour before the Duchess arrived, with the dignitaries mingling outside, Derek arrived. He understood the situation and we settled him into bed and welcomed his wife Jessie with him.

This really is two stories in one, for after receiving the Duchess at the door of the hospice and after she had done her curtain pulling on the commemorative plaque, I took our guest round the patients. This was the Duchess who not long afterwards withdrew from the royal circle, and as Katherine Worsley again, taught piano and followed a devout Christian pattern of life. It was in keeping that she had asked only to meet patients and not spend much time with the invited guests. She spoke to Phoebe at great length.

When she came to Derek, I explained the situation and she realised how recently he had arrived in the hospice, and the gravity of his condition. She told him the story of the footprints in the sand, which I hope is familiar to readers. It ends, "My son, that is when I was carrying you." Derek cried, Jessie cried, the Duchess cried, and Joy and I cried.

What to do with a crying Duchess? I took her to our bathroom with its jacuzzi bath. She wiped her eyes at the mirror. "Did I overdo it?" she asked. I assured her that her words would be a comfort and remembered long after that day.

Derek's first day with us was exceptional. Following examination of him, I realised why no surgeon had tackled this ugly rectal cancer. Derek, an articulate, highly intelligent man confessed that life was not worth living in his present situation. I put it to him that if I could persuade a surgeon to operate, the risk of him dying at the time of surgery was grave. He replied he would rather die on the operating table than continue the painful undignified existence he had to suffer daily.

I contacted a Bart's trained surgeon whom I had known whilst employed at Bart's myself. Hearing the full story, he agreed to come to see Derek at Oakhaven. They talked at length and as he left surgeon Chris said, "Jan, I'll do it for you." I could not thank him enough.

The outcome was, that Derek had the surgery which left him with a colostomy but restored comfort and dignity. He came back to us in early summer to recuperate and then was followed up at home. So much for his original estimate of death within days of admission. That Christmas he was home with family in Cape Town and swam in the sea!

He died the following summer, a gentle death in which we were able to support both Derek and Jessie. No-one should tell another how long they have to live. The implications are too grave and are inaccurate.

Another patient I will never forget was a single woman in her fifties, who was an accountant. A tough character who had led a successful independent life but seemed short of family support and local friends. She appreciated what the hospice could give her, privacy, courtesy, specialist care and good-humoured conversation. I spent many out of hours time getting to know her. Her main distress from her cancer was shortness of breath. It was late one evening when I was called as she was asking for me. The constant breathlessness was exhausting to her. "Am I dying?" she asked. Knowing her so well I knew my reply would be understood. "I hope so" I said, "For this is no way to be alive." "Beam me up Scottie" she said and died within minutes. It was almost as if she wanted my agreement and approval of her wish to die.

The privilege of sharing time with the dying is one not given to many, and indeed, some find it difficult and frightening. However, coming to terms with death, others and one's own is an important part of living a full life. The unknown question to which not even the greatest intellect has the answer should not be viewed with fear but with curiosity for a new adventure. Joyous, or an anti-climax? We will never know.

Over the eight years of first planning and then running Oakhaven as its Medical Director, many memorable events come to mind, but none more valuable than the privilege of getting to know people at the end of life. Time is so precious then. There were several social occasions I had to share, but they pale into insignificance compared with the one to one times with these patients, many of whom became friends. Their families too were special to us and were part of our hospice family in their bereavement.

Joy and I, with our husbands, attended a Royal Garden Party at Buckingham Palace, representing the hospice. I have since read that the party invitation is a recompense for those who miss out on an OBE! It was an interesting day, and one my husband did not find to his liking, but supported me, as always, in agreeing to attend. He was I suppose, the introvert to my extrovert personality but we combined well. He would not have been involved unless he knew my need for his help. It was out of keeping that having been irritated beyond measure by the top hatted equerries with their rolled umbrellas, herding us masses like sheep round the palace lawn, he spoke up at an opportune moment. We were well away from the royalty followers watching members of The Family, speaking with the chosen selected few members of the public.

Prince Charles spent longer than most engaging in conversation with these people, much to the annoyance of the equerries, who wanted the Royals on time for tea with the Queen. Charles eventually came down the lawn towards us. As he approached us, being a good Quaker for whom all are equal, I did not lower my gaze. He came over to Greville and myself and commented that we were lucky that the weather had stayed fine. Much to my surprise Greville replied, "Not half so lucky but that you have welcomed us. May I introduce my wife, she's a doctor." I was dumbstruck to hear this from my retiring husband.

Charles then asked if we were both doctors, and Greville explained about Oakhaven. He asked me much about the hospice and was obviously well aware of the financial situation when I told him of our charitable status, and how much we had to raise each year. Then he surprised me by saying quietly, so only I could hear, "I don't think I'd cope with cancer." "You would cope very well from what I see" I replied. With a pat on my shoulder, he replied, "I think you're marvellous!" Good gracious. The nearest I'd get to being dubbed with a sword.

Meanwhile, Joy and I were trying to fulfil a request from our Day Centre patients who knew of our outing to the Palace. They wanted us to bring back a royal cucumber sandwich. A simple request you may think, but difficult in the circumstances. We selected our sandwiches from the amazing tea tent, and quietly slipped one each into our handbags, wrapped in paper napkins.

At the end of our exciting day, I examined my cucumber sandwich. To my dismay, it was egg mayonnaise and a bit of a mess. However, Joy's fitted the bill and was taken ceremonially to the Day Centre at lunch time next day. Much admired by the patients, but unceremoniously scoffed by Charlie, the PAT dog of Marilyn, the Centre's supervisor. Cling film, paper plate and all, whilst we were at lunch! So we have no record of the day, just a stain on the carpet.

A regular visitor to the Day Centre as a patient was a petite lady, Grace. It seems cruel that someone who for most of her life had been severely disabled with rheumatoid arthritis should also develop carcinoma as well. Grace was a Quaker like myself, and lived in Quaker House, a residential home in New Milton. She had been wheelchair bound for many years before we met her. Small she may have been, but she was great in wisdom. It was a delight to have her visit on a regular basis. She wrote poetry and sometimes left some at the hospice for us. I include one in her memory. She died in 1995, aged 80.

Blake said joy and woe are intertwined,
And this today is on my mind.
Kind eyes meet mine along the way
And gentle words are spoken too,
Reminding me that, every day
You may need me, as I need you.
For joy is when you show your care for me
And woe is when your pain I fail to see.
And so, today I pray to quiet be
That I may know your need
To be much greater than my own.
The love of God lets no-one be alone.

Even more sad than elderly deaths were those of the young. Some leaving behind young families to be cared for by a single parent, or indeed taken into care by strangers. One such was a young woman with two school age children, who discovered she had a breast cancer during the early days of her third pregnancy. She kept the fact of pregnancy from her doctor until it was too late for a termination. Soon after the baby was born, she came under our care. It was about three months later that her husband a lorry driver suddenly died of a heart attack. She struggled on bringing up her children with a little family support, but mostly help from a friend who would take the children off her hands to give her a break. The inevitable deterioration in her health as the cancer became more aggressive meant that we saw more of her at Oakhaven. Social services had become involved at an earlier stage via the GP. We were very concerned for the family's future after mother's death and shared our thoughts and actions with social services. The mother's dearest wish was that her three orphans would be able to grow up together. Their mother was heroic. At no time did she show concern for herself. Living permanently now in the hospice, she thought only of her children. A very kind friend took on the majority of childcare. Social services found a couple who were teachers. Childless, they expressed a wish to adopt, and slowly became more involved as mother's condition deteriorated.

During her last months, she had put together a special tape which was to be a keepsake for the children to remember Mum. After all, this was all they would have as years went by.

When mother died, the teacher couple with help from social services and the friend, took the children. The eldest, a girl at secondary school locally, saw herself as responsible for her two siblings. Arrangements quickly broke down when the adoptive couple said they could not cope. There was resentment of the role the eldest child perceived she should have with her brother and sister.

The children were split up, going to a couple some

distance from Lymington, making visits by the elder sister to the younger ones impossible without help. The elder girl remained at comprehensive school locally and stayed with the staunch family friend. This teenager was quite a character and showed it by walking into a local solicitor's office and seeking advice on the family situation. Social services had been unsupportive to the girl, and she was not able to be involved with her siblings.

Eventually the case went to court. Social Services were criticised for the management of the case. The judge asked what had happened to the lifeline tape made by the mother with such care. The social worker's reply was somewhat casual when she said she thought it was in the glove box of her car. What unkindness. Access for the family to spend time together was the outcome, but I wonder if it did actually succeed. I do not know the end of the story, but that big sister deserved the best.

Fund raising in these early days had to be done by anyone willing to help. I gathered around me some outstandingly generous folk, both financially and in time and energy.

Soon after all five beds were opened and nursing staff appointed, when finance allowed, I did my first Oakhaven Challenge to raise the cost of a nurse for a year in one day. Like so many things having significant outcome for the hospice, it happened by chance.

We ate lunch in the early days in restaurant style with the day centre patients. We had a cook who made wonderful lemon meringue pies. Marilyn, in charge of the day centre, finishing off a slice saying, "I could eat a whole one of those." To which I replied, "I'll keep you to that." Never known to miss a challenge Marilyn said, "If I do that, what will you do?" Without much thought I said, "I'll stand on my head and sing God Save the Queen!" Conversation ended with much laughter but driving home I thought "that's not a bad idea. It costs nothing and I've always been able to stand on my head". Out of this episode came a wonderful local event, my Challenge to Lymington to raise the cost of a nurse for a year in one day by doing something silly costing nothing. This struck a chord. I challenged everyone via newspapers, local flyers and radio. For this challenge I would stand on my head on the steps of Moore and Blatch, a notable solicitors office in a Georgian building in the town at twelve noon and sing the National Anthem. "What will you do?"

So many took up the silly challenge. Bank managers, estate agents and lawyers had wet sponges thrown at them whilst in the stocks. Many schools took part. I managed for the first time ever to get approval to get the High Street closed from the Parish Church for over two hundred yards, to do silly things in the evening of that day. A master of one school allowed people, mainly his pupils, to play Russian Roulette with eggs, by smashing them on his head. About one in ten was not hard boiled and 'sir' was a pretty sight. A good yolk. A worthy elderly couple solemnly measured the length of the High Street with a yard-long sausage. All recorded by the wife on a clip board, as her husband grovelled along the kerb. A pair of goats was taken into the more elegant shops, whose owners were happy to put money in the bucket to get them outside before they did a whoopsie. One firm of solicitors, with senior partner dressed as the Mad Hatter, held an Alice in Wonderland tea party outside their office. Phoebe Coates took part, unrecognised, dressed as a gypsy flower seller. My daughter, with guitar, and a friend with saxophone, sat on the kerb edge playing with a notice beside them 'Give us some money to go away.' After my challenge, the local WI groups raised several hundred pounds sitting in shop doorways knitting. They knitted two blankets from squares that evening, which were useful at the hospice. The fire brigade and bus service both got involved. A bus load of children was pulled down the street by the fire brigade.

Meanwhile, I was challenged to stand on my head thirteen times – in shops, restaurants, in the hospice itself, always dressed as a clown.

I raised £1,300 and yes, we did raise the cost of a nurse for a year in one day. The Challenge happened twice more, on alternate years, but no longer after I retired in 1996. Medical Directors after my time were not inclined to involve themselves in anything other than medicine. No fund raising, no social networking. These things were left to paid employees. Our frugal budget at the outset made it necessary for me to promote Oakhaven in any way I could. I have just remembered a challenge from that day. Many people abseiled down the church tower.

The Hospice legal team collected disclaimers for injury at the foot of the tower, and the Vicar of Lymington prayed for them at the top, as they launched themselves over the wall.

Fund raising has become a big organisation now for the hospice and very vital. Bigger events involving many people and many parts of the globe occur, and raise funds even more necessary than before, as costs in every department increase yearly. What started with a quarter of a million pounds, a croquet lawn and a few committed people now needs millions of pounds a year to continue bringing free care to all in need of its expertise. Very many more jobs have been created, and I am no longer actively involved.

It was sad for me in some ways to leave something I had created, but in 1996 I felt that at 62 I should retire as Medical Director. It was time to go. I had been in dispute for over a year with the trustees about my salary, and I was tired of fighting my corner. Because I started in a part-time capacity, they felt that was the salary I deserved, yet they knew that for me it was a full-time job. It was financially expedient for them to save money this way. The whole thing was distasteful, and I was relieved to step aside. Administration was rearing its head. Earlier, the trustees in a very disgraceful way had discussed the removal of our current administrator, Ray, whilst he took the minutes of the meeting. His post was to change to a full time one with the more grandiose title of chief executive. I was present at that meeting and could not believe what I was hearing. Ray, who came from the post of bursar at Kingston University, had done a first class job and was hard working and well liked. Not so his successor whom the Trust appointed. She was in post when I retired. I learned from my secretary that she was angry when she found out how much money had been collected for my leaving gifts, and she had not been involved. I of course knew little of this until well after the event. She moved in clumsily telling me that I was to compile a list of folk to be invited to my leaving party at a local timeshare establishment, Elmers Court. This was certainly not my wish at all. I had in mind an evening out with my staff. She made it into a much more public occasion with people I would never have invited. When she heard that my chosen gifts; an armchair, a desk and several other items had been earmarked, she said they were not suitable and told my secretary to buy me pearls. I had no wish for such a gift and made it known to my staff. At the leaving event, the joke was on the lady, for my senior nurse handed out pearls to all the nursing team, to wear at the farewell party, as I did too.

Eight years of my life had been devoted to establishing the Hospice, thanks to the generosity of Phoebe Coates, and I look back over twenty-five years later with modest pride upon what I was able to achieve with the support and kindness of so many who have over the years become my friends.

Oakhaven's first medical director

1996

Coming Home

So began another chapter of my life. More self-indulgent, more family orientated and with much less responsibility. I still had connections with Oakhaven but my contact with patients was no more, and this I missed so much.

One of the episodes coming into the did I really do that? category was my two weeks in Moscow, teaching palliative care under the auspices of the British Russian Hospice Society.

Two years after retirement from Oakhaven I was contacted by this Society and invited to join with three other medics specialising in care of the dying, to teach at the first Moscow Hospice for two weeks. The Hospice had been formally opened by the wife of the Mayor of Moscow, Luzhkov, the day before we started our teaching. We each had topics to focus upon. Mine was alternative therapies, and the influence of environment on the patient's wellbeing. This proved to be of great significance in Russia, where hospice care was almost basic compared with that we were familiar with at home. We learned as much in our stay in Moscow as any of the 17 participants who came from far flung regions of this vast country, and who had so little materially to offer their patients. We were constantly surprised by the questions and comments of our audience in our lectures.

Some of the treatments one would describe as primitive and even, once or twice, downright dangerous. For example, "If you have one tablet of 10 mg diamorphine, when would you give it?" Or "Would you use kerosene to relieve pain in carcinoma of the stomach?" We were aware of the underlying poverty which led to the methods of care given to the dying patient. Such a complex country as Russia made it difficult to advise the doctor who had travelled thousands of miles to be at the Moscow hospice. The hospice itself was far behind anything we would expect in the UK. It was a converted building, and it would be easy to criticise the transition to a hospice, but so many obvious necessities were missing. A great deal of money had been spent on items which were of fringe benefit. An example of the political influence was the inclusion of a chapel, complete with gold onion-domed roof. This apparently was on the instruction of the mayor of Moscow who had, for his political advancement, got behind the planning of the building, financing this chapel and insisting on the golden dome. Yet not providing for basics of privacy and comfort for patients.

President Putin has harnessed the Russian Orthodox religion into his ambitious plans for the country and the Moscow mayor was in thrall to him. The rebuilding, of an exact replica of the original Cathedral in Moscow, was evidence of how the emerging religious revival was done to influence the state.

We had an example of the part faith played in the practice of care of the dying when one of our team visited a small apartment where a woman was in an advanced stage of breast cancer. She was asked by our team member what she did for pain control. There was an icon on the wall at the foot of her bed. She nodded at it. "That is my pain relief" she said.

The doctors themselves were in alien territory, coming from far distant parts of the vast country. Unfortunately, their lack of english and our ignorance of russian made it difficult to make meaningful friendships with our Russian colleagues. An interpreter was always needed. We had a farewell gathering which they had funded. Many of our audience were paid a pittance for devotion to their work. Indeed, some had not been paid for months. The trip to Moscow was more of a publicity effort for their superiors locally. The offering in farewell that they were able to fund amounted to a box of chocolates to share and a bottle of local sparkling wine which they called champagne.

In conversation I observed that I would be home in 24 hours. The doctor next to me woefully said when she boarded the train that evening, she had 2½ days on board before she reached her home in Siberia. We cannot easily imagine the enormity of the country.

On my return I gave one or two talks of my experiences in Moscow, but always felt it difficult to impress my audience with the contrasts in so many aspects of the trip.

Whilst I was in practice and Greville was teaching, our time for holidays was limited, but in retirement time was not the important factor. It is pleasing to reminisce on the past pleasant experiences from our holiday times together.

Sunshine in Paros

Unintentionally, when looking back, I find that we sought holiday places on islands, for example Mull, Bryher and Alderney. Even as I write, at 86 I am on the Greek Island of Alonnisos. We had always loved all things Greek, and soon after we married, we holidayed in 1973 on the island of Rhodes. An island then far removed from the commercialism of today. This taste for Greece stayed with us and over the 45 years of our marriage the call of Greece, mostly the Aegean islands remained strong.

Our greatest joy for so many years came from these visits to Greece. We had both been enchanted by this country's ancient history, architecture and culture from our time at sea, and now we could visit and learn more of the modern country we grew to love. Not only did we visit more than ten Aegean Islands, but also explored varied parts of the mainland, from Mount Athos in the north to the Venetian castle at Methoni in the Southern Peloponnese. My favourite place on earth I have decided is Delphi. This is appropriate really because the ancient Greeks thought it was the omphalos or navel, birthplace of the world. I have sat high in the hills in the amphitheatre at Delphi, at 5.30 a.m., alone, sun rising, with the cliffs of Mount Parnassus above me with eagles circling on high relishing the silence and magic of this place. I am such a lucky person.

But the special group of islands for us, since being recommended by a colleague at the hospice, has been the Sporades. These very green islands in the northern Aegean are close to the mainland, unspoiled by tourism. Further south the climate is hotter and the architecture less pleasing to us, in the Cyclades or Dodecanese Islands to the east. It was in 1994 that we first landed on Skiathos, the only island in the group to have an airport. We were enchanted by the happiness of the islanders and by the scenery. Sandy beaches in abundance, blue warm sea and small places in which to stay. Predictably, the island has become very popular with all foreigners, especially Brits, and is now spoilt by tourism. However, it is the gateway to the two other islands we grew to love over the next twenty-five years, Skopelos and Alonnisos. They are far less able to be over commercialised because they are more difficult to get to. Ferry journeys must follow the 3½ hour flight from the UK. When money was available to Greece on joining the EU, it was proposed to build a runway on Skopelos. In their wisdom they turned the offer down, thus protecting the character of the island. It is an island where the main town and port welcomes you with its cluster of small houses and churches huddled together on a steep hillside rising up from the waterside. In the many times we stayed on Skopelos, we have got to know the inhabitants and admire their uncomplicated way of life. Children we met as toddlers, we now see grown into attractive adults studying at universities throughout the mainland.

One charming small house we stayed in many times, high up, alone in the hills, had 13 different types of fruit trees from carob and lemon to pomegranate and apricot and, of course, with its own olive grove. Its owner Spiros, and family of Maria his wife, and daughter Angelika are still our friends. The islands are popular with the sailing fraternity, although I understand because of prevailing winds and the summer's meltemi, sailing is sometimes tricky.

We began sharing our holidays between Skopelos and its near neighbour, Alonnisos. People in the know would say, "Skopelos is quiet, but Alonnisos is much quieter," and this we came to agree and enjoy.

We first stayed on Alonnisos in 1998 in a tiny house high above the port of Patitiri, but within walking distance. We walked everywhere at that time and got to know the port and the old town, the Chora, standing as a sentinel on a high point of the island. In olden days a look out for islanders for marauding Turkish pirates. Sadly in 1965, the Chora, where the majority of the islanders lived, was destroyed by an earthquake. This changed the island in many ways. It brought great distress as many were made homeless and lived in tents for over a year, including through the hard winter weather. Now the port of Patitiri is the only place with sufficient facilities to run the island, having its schooling, administration and medical care centred there.

The island bewitched us over the next quarter of a century, calling us back year on year until it seems like a second home. Some of our happiest times were spent on Alonnisos, and now, after Greville's death in 2017, it has given solace to me. Although when there alone sometimes yet I am never lonely. Friendships made here have been long lasting and important.

We visited first of all through a travel operator, Greek Islands Club. Through them we rented our holiday home then called Amalia. When staying in a house high above Tzortsi Bay, whilst swimming in the bay I looked up to where a very pretty bougainvillea covered terrace of a white single storey house was sited very close to the water. It was to one side of the bay on its own, and the only house close to the sea. It had its own slipway into the water and was about 100 yards up an unmade track leading only to this house.

Spiti Federico, Tzortsi Bay, Alonnisos

To our delight the next year, we found this house Amalia was available to rent from our agents. Although at that time it was not in good condition and the furnishings were worn, we fell in love with the tranquillity of its position and the beauty of the bay. Apart from the yachts coming to anchor overnight in the summer months, Tzortsi was ours, no-one in sight, although some houses were dotted around the hillside behind us. The sheltered terrace at the front of the house looked down onto the rocky coast twenty yards below. A single storey blue and white fisherman's hut was close to shore within the grounds of the house. Terraces stretched down to the path below, each with mature olive, orange and lemon trees and pink oleander.

Each year from that first visit we came to Amalia even

though it was shabby. We learnt from our contact on Alonnisos, dear Julia Browne, that the owners were German and that they had their own house on the Island. Sadly, the owner's wife was in the terminal stages of cancer and so she and her husband had not been to Alonnisos for some time.

That was until 2010 when we heard from our friend, Kostas Mavrikis, that the owner was on the Island with an architect and would probably be coming to Amalia. We learned that the owner's wife had died, and he was possibly going to sell the house.

Sure enough the owner did visit as we were having breakfast on the terrace. As he came up the path, we noticed that he had a blonde lady with him. He said, "May we come in?" To which Greville replied, "I think it is your house? Of course you can come in."

We were introduced to this tall, well built German gentleman wearing a panama hat. He clicked his heels and bowed. The lady stepped forward and introduced herself as Elenore. They had come to see the house, which Elenore was persuading Friedrich Popken, for that was our visitor's name, not to sell.

We then heard the romantic story of this couple. As teenage and early twenties youngsters they met when learning english in London. Although possibly romantically involved they went their separate ways but kept in touch. Friedrich joined the family retail business in Hamelin in northern Germany, having married his wife Ursula on return to his homeland. The business flourished, first with maternity and baby clothes, and later with outsize ladies garments. They had a boy and girl, who were in their middle age by the time we met Friedrich.

Meanwhile Elenore married an Italian banker and lived in Rome. When her two boys were at university her husband died suddenly of a heart attack, leaving her a widow for seventeen years.

When Friedrich's wife died, he decided to visit Rome to call on Elenore. He was told that she was in Germany. He had gone looking for her, as she looked for him. They were engaged in three weeks and married in three months. A true love story.

Elenore had great plans for restoring Amalia making it another holiday home for the new families, together with the house at Tripiti which Friedrich's first wife Ulla had had built many years earlier.

I asked, "And will you still let this house through Greek Islands Club?" "Oh no," said Elenore, "it will be for the family." At once Friedrich looked at me and said, "Jan, I know you love this place. I saw your face. You can stay whenever you like!" So began a very happy friendship with this couple which has been a significant part of our following years, allowing us to plan stays in Spiti Federico each year since that time. In 2011 the house was reborn and is now a very attractive spacious villa on its own in Tzortsi Bay so close to the sea. From its own slipway and steps, we can plop into the blue sea, or sunbathe on beds on the promontory above. Time passes gently and life is uncomplicated, allowing us to restore our energies for the winter to come in England.

Friedrich is a charming, warm hearted, generous businessman.

Friedrich and Elenore Popken came to lunch

Over time we learned of his extensive clothing business in France and Germany. When I asked what airline they used to fly home, the reply from Elenore, "My son comes to get us in the plane!" In another conversation the 'schloss' was mentioned. Friedrich owns a seventeenth century castle which he has developed into a five-star hotel, Hotel Munchausen, near Hanover.

Hotel Munchausen

In 2019 the Popkens invited some friends of mine, whom they had met on Alonnisos to join me for a weekend at this stunning hotel. Before I could consider how we would all get from Lymington to Germany, Friedrich said, "And we'll come and get you in the plane." What a wonderful weekend we spent.

On Alonnisos the Popkens had an extensive property overlooking the sea, where Greville and I shared even more hospitality. My visitors and I were invited to join them and their boatman Iannis, and Kostas and Angela Mavrikis, on trips on their 900 horsepower boat. A special visit, on two occasions, was to the Island of Skiros, known as the burial place of poet Rupert Brooke. There we met Dimitri a taverna owner, a dear man who had an English wife. Sadly, she had lung cancer at the time of our first visit. When we next visited Dimitri was greatly distressed, for it was the anniversary of his wife's death the year before. To celebrate her life, he gave us the carcass of a goat to take back to Kostas' family restaurant at Steni Vala on Alonnisos, with the request that we have a party in his wife's memory. The goat was tough, but the wine was smooth, and celebration went on late into the night at Tassia's taverna. Greville had died before this episode in our friendship with the Popkens, but I know he would have enjoyed the event so much.

One unusual and not altogether successful trip to Greece was with Great Rail Journeys in 2013. We joined Eurostar at Waterloo and then travelled by rail through Europe, ending up in Athens for the last four days of our trip. "Fourteen days to get there, and four hours to get back" was Greville's observation as we flew home. All a bit overwhelming and too busy compared with our tranquil days on Alonnisos. More for railway enthusiasts than Grecofiles we concluded. However, it gave us, in two weeks, a chance to see once more so many of the sites we had visited in our youth when at sea. Patras, Olympia, Corinth, Mycenae, Epidaurus and, of course, Athens.

I love Greece and would be happy to have some of my ashes scattered in the waters of Tzortsi Bay in Alonnisos but not yet.

All Good Things

Our summer days on Alonnisos together came to an end in 2015. For some time, I had noticed that Greville's memory was deteriorating. When one has lived so closely to each other for over 40 years little changes in behaviour can be missed. When I did feel that cognition was becoming a problem in mid 2014, Greville saw a psychiatrist who diagnosed mild cognitive impairment.

The mild was to become more serious that year and in January 2015 Greville was admitted to hospital having had a stroke, leaving him with vascular dementia. Whilst able to walk and talk in those early days, his ability to understand what was needed of him was poor. Not only that, but also because of renal problems, he had been self-catheterising twice daily for two years. This task from then on fell to me, so I could never be away from him for long. I extracted him from the local hospital, had a stairlift installed and brought him home to Pilley. Our lives changed. As in his life he was less and less able to understand and co-operate, so mine became more and more committed to his care. For nearly three years I watched the dementia overcome him. His mobility diminished until he could only walk a few steps with a zimmer frame, then used a wheelchair.

He lost all interest in anything which previously he had enjoyed. He could not understand anything in the newspaper. All his senses were affected with this evil disease. At first, I did not register that his sense of taste and smell had gone. This I gather is an early sign of progressive dementia. Eyesight and hearing were also affected. Poor chap, his days were empty of anything of interest to him. He would seem contented however. When I asked, "Is anything worrying you?" "Are you anxious about anything?" He would reply, "No, why should I be?" I knew he trusted me to care for him, but who I was, as time went by, he was not sure. He would stare hard at me and say, "Is it Jan?" I would reply, "Yes, and it has been for over 40 years." "Oh." End of conversation.

As it became harder to care for him, I had the help of the Hospice's Care Agency. While Oakhaven offered free service to its patients, the Care Agency was developed as a paid service, with any profits being ploughed into Oakhaven funds. It became very expensive to have help in getting him up and dressed in the morning. Help with bathing again was vital. If I had four hours off once a week, it cost £80 for a carer to be in the house with him.

To keep my sanity in this existence I resolved to still take a break on Alonnisos each year. This was restorative. Except on one occasion when I invited a couple who had been my colleagues on school ships to share Spiti Federico with me. I did not realise how creaky they were, and spent the holiday caring for them, only to return to do the same again with Greville at home. He went into a nursing home when I had a break and he hated it. "My wife should be doing this" he would say to staff as they tended to him.

It was inevitable with his immobility and anorexia that

his physical condition deteriorated as well as his cognition.

I say with sincerity that I can only think 'Thank God' when he died gently at home in his own bed on July 22nd, 2017. An excellent Oakhaven carer was on a routine morning visit at the time. We were both at his bedside as he slipped his mortal coil and moved on to – who knows?

I had tried my best to make his last days tolerable. In the announcement of his death in the Times, we wrote "He died gently and untroubled". I hope this was true.

Jenny was very helpful. Although she and Richard lived fairly close at hand in Southbourne, with two small children visiting was limited. Jenny and Greville had always been close and loved each other dearly but with little demonstrative affection. I knew how alike in temperament they were. Two only children who in many ways had had to find their own amusement with working parents. Sometimes I have felt Jenny was deprived by my professional life and I deeply regret that.

A thanksgiving service at St John the Baptist Church, Boldre brought together both the three daughters of his first marriage and also his first wife Lyndi with Jenny and myself. We have had little contact since, however. Greville is buried in woodland in designated land at Hinton, about 15 miles from home. A guelder rose grows over his plot and seasonal bulbs spring up over the year. A gentle place suitable for a gentleman. We were married for nearly 45 years.

2017

Going Solo With Memories to Cherish

Bereavement is a special time in one's life and needs to be regarded as such. I always felt myself catching my breath when relatives, revisiting the hospice after the death of a loved one, would say, especially of the widow, "She was wonderful, she was back at work the next week." Time to mourn is vital, a special part of the time of grief. My recollection of this time however is different. For three years I had lost Greville and lived through this time, bereaved but unable to mourn, for this dear man was dead to me, but still with me and dependent upon me. It was hard.

Such an experience also gives one greater insight into one's relationships, not only in the family, but also with those whom one had known as friends over the years. A great eye-opener. On reflection I think I had mis-read some folk who deserted me as Greville's condition worsened. One visit was enough for them. When Greville did not respond and had no conversation, they did not return. A real "I don't know what to say" episode. I had had such a time with Phoebe Coates when her friends deserted her as her dementia left her as an empty shell. I would say to them, "Just be there, don't worry about lack of conversation." I'm sure the presence of recognised people must give some comfort and reassurance.

I took my time after Greville's death to re-establish a

gentle routine. It was no longer necessary to keep an ear alert to be able to care when needed. No longer the need to get up two or three times a night, to put back the pillows and duvets on the floor or coax him back to bed when wandering. I was grateful for the peace I had missed for so long. I found myself still declining invitations for in my mind I was still needed at home all hours of the day or night. By the beginning of 2018 I was ready to start again but going solo. This really has to be thought through. Although I had been without companionship for some time, I was now aware of the emptiness of the armchair opposite me by the fireside, and the intensity of the feeling of loneliness that at times overcame me.

I resolved to make something out of what was left, and find the creative attitude needed to be happy. I hope I have done this. Writing the history of one's life so far is part of that. When one is aware that there is inevitably so much more living behind you than, at 86, one can have before you, it is important to look back with gratitude and forward with hope. So much I have experienced and so many episodes in my life have brought me a sense of satisfaction. "Did I really do that?" "I'm so glad I met them." "I shall always remember that day or days." "I have been so fortunate."

Retirement is pleasurable if one is in good health and financially secure. Since I, fortunately, found myself in this category I enjoyed many new interests, especially those that Greville and I could share.

As firm supporters of Salisbury Playhouse we were regularly to be found in our sponsored seats at their matinee performances. A terrific provincial theatre deserving of success. The variety of its programme widened our interest in playwrights we had only come across on television previously, if at all.

I had always enjoyed the stage, and had fun locally with our village group, The Pilley Players. Minor roles and some script writing helped to fill dark winter evenings.

We had a number of years as members of Chewton Glen lunch club. This five-star hotel was a joy to visit, not just for the delicious lunches, but the overall experience of gracious living.

I love Greece and would be happy to have some of my ashes scattered in Alonnisos at Tzortsi Bay, whilst the rest join with Greville at the Woodland Burial Ground. But not yet!

My account of life in retirement has not really been in chronological order. Just written down as things come to mind and wondering how much more I have got to write as the years go by. At 86 it seems amazing to me that it is now twenty years since I completed my part time two years MA course at Reading University. It was entitled 'Death and Society.' It was directed by a lecturer in the Sociology Department, Tony Walter.

I saw an advertisement in the Times, announcing this unusual MA course. When I saw the syllabus, I was enthused to apply. There were nine of us in all who studied the topics, which all related to some aspect of death. When one thinks about it, all of life leads to study of death if only remotely. We looked into sociology, religion, architecture, archaeology, history, medicine and anthropology, all focussing on their relationship with death. We were all mature students and came from very varied walks of life. One, a fifth generation funeral director from the east end of London, kept us more than a little amused with his black humour, as well as giving us insight into the diverse aspects of his chosen profession. Funerals for so many communities in the East End of London had to be addressed and all rituals observed. Some were to European eyes very strange. Who would put a pig's head or money in a coffin? The old fashioned horse drawn hearse, now the acme of respectability for some local families, was catered for by these funeral directors, who had magnificent black horses with plumed head gear, and the grooms all impressively turned out. We visited the funeral parlour and marvelled at the enormous lead lined coffins which would be despatched round the world, often to the Middle East or America. We visited cathedrals, archaeological digs, studied archive material and searched in libraries and museums.

It was a challenge to me, who had not written an essay for over forty years, but I found the intellectual stimulus of the course rewarding. Whilst some of my fellow students were rather earnest and intense, there was a nucleus of light-hearted, amusing individuals who made the sessions acceptable. One criticism would be that, for what we had paid in fees, there was minimal professional teaching. At some stages we felt our knowledge, from experience, was greater than our tutors. Three of us came from medical background, whilst one was an archivist, another a clergyman and another conducted humanist funerals.

We were required to write a 20,000 + word dissertation to gain our degree. I focussed on my Quaker faith and entitled it 'Quakers, where do we go from here?' Being a non-credal religion I explored thoughts on other worlds and the belief in an afterlife. I was really I suppose challenging myself and my beliefs whilst exploring the beliefs of others whom I interviewed. It was a good two years and although I am not in touch with any of my fellow students, I think of them with affection. During my research I visited Woodbrooke, the Quaker section of Birmingham University, which is housed in the home of the distinguished Quaker family, the Cadburys at Bourneville. There I met many committed Quakers, very diverse in background, outlook and thought. All stimulating company, and people I have grown to like and respect. Although I felt very different from many I met there, I was always comfortable in their presence.

I was much involved with the local Quaker meeting at this time in the 1990s. Having been energised by the Friends I had met at Woodbrooke more and more I found that any ministry in my local Meeting did not speak to me, and that I valued the silence above anything else. I agree with the observation of Prince Philip on long sermons quoted at the time of his death. "The mind cannot absorb what the backside cannot endure." Having been attending regularly since I first worshipped with the Lymington Quakers in 1983, I no longer felt inspired to join in when I had the life changing experience of looking after Greville after his stroke in January 2013. I made a wrong assumption that my friends within the churches of all denominations in Lymington would be my supporters. This did not turn out to be so. Having, say, visited Greville once and found there was no conversation and little recognition, most rarely came again. Greville had worshipped at the Lymington Parish Church for years, but only once did the vicar phone in nearly three years, and never visited. It was as if we didn't count. (These 'unchristian' thoughts have troubled me).

The kindnesses came from neighbours and from unexpected sources. One kindness I shall always be grateful for was that of Steve, the excellent chef and proprietor of the local pub, the Fleur de Lys. He had always said, "Jan, give me a call if you want me." So had others, but never came. Not so Steve. In the middle of Steve's busy Sunday lunch service, Greville had fallen to the floor in the living room and I could not get him up. Calling an ambulance, I had learned was a long drawn-out business for which one had to wait. I called Steve. "I'll be there in a minute." And sure enough, in his chef's garb, in the middle of Sunday lunches, he dropped everything and came. Not only did he lift Greville gently back into his chair, but he waited with him to see he was settled and comfortable. That was the good Samaritan we read about in the Bible. "Who is my neighbour?" That Sunday lunch time I had the answer to that question.

My exploration of my faith moved away from any denominational religion. Much of association with such a group of worshippers is more a construct of man than of God. From the political influences of the time of

Christ's life on earth to those of today I observed that power has been the motive of those leading the church. For me, my relationship with the concept of 'God' is personal and does not need earthly trappings of any kind.

The Quakers were as near to that concept as I could find, but yet again, within the Quaker Meeting one was obliged to focus on ministry of those around one rather than the God within.

After my experience when caring for Greville I found, more and more, that I needed to be on my own to seek to know that of God. This may be selfish, but I can serve God in other ways rather than within a denominational religion. It also allows me to respect all faiths and find my place within them.

I found this first leader in the Times 23.12.06. 'There is a confusion today over the contradiction between conviction and convention. Much of what we take as the essence of faith is really only tradition, an inheritance from the past and a comforting, historical continuity.' This I believe to be so. In the last years of my life, I am content to recognise how fortunate I am to have access to a building in which I can spend some time alone seeking that of God. This building is the local Anglican church, St John the Baptist, Boldre, nearly a thousand years old. Its present priest in charge is easy to talk to, unphased by my need to use the beautiful building, whilst not accepting the manner of worship it represents.

One of my most pleasing times in my 86th year is spent,

first, swimming a quarter of a mile in the local spa, and then, on the way home calling into St John the Baptist Church for my time in which to seek God.

Thirty seven years in the village of Pilley in the New Forest has been a joy. The small, terraced house we were able to buy with a mortgage, in the eighties has increased in value many times over, but most houses in the village now command a price of nearly a million pounds. To have the New Forest on the doorstep is a great selling point. Being in the National Park means that we are protected from further house building locally. In Lymington itself in 2020 there is great demand for expansion of the town. In the New Forest we do not have that demand. Our concern is to keep the character of the village whilst second home buyers, mainly from London, aim to snap up any house coming on the market. There is a good corporate feel to the community, which is maintained mostly by the involvement of the village shop and post office. Whereas in years past the hub for villagers would revolve around the church, in these secular days the village shop is that meeting point. As a not for profit community enterprise we feel we have an interest in the shop's success, being shareholders. The shop is a meeting place, a source of support for any needy members of the village and is always in demand since the Post Office is housed within the shop.

Although I retired from Oakhaven in 1996 I continued to keep in contact with many staff members and the chief executive although only occasionally visiting them. I made great friends with the girls in the fund-raising office. They find ways of collecting money for the hospice throughout the year. The service given to patients and their relatives is free. This means that the need to raise funds for all departments of the hospice must continue, year in, year out. Only 17% of funding comes from government sources, the rest being up to local effort. The fundraising office is always looking for ways to raise the money to maintain Oakhaven's work both within the hospice and out in the community.

To help in this way I offered to do a sky dive on my 85th birthday, September 6th, 2019.

My tandem escorts me to the plane

Tipped out above the clouds

I was booked for this date at the Army Parachute Association's premises at Netheravon, north of Salisbury. Owing to weather conditions, I actually did the jump the following day. Even then, the sky was quite cloudy, but suitable for the planes to take us up above 14,000 feet. Jill, from the fundraising office took me to the jump zone, where I had to sign a disclaimer for any injury before paying my fee, getting kitted out in overalls and helmet before a time of instruction in the gym. "Don't do anything until you hear the instruction shouted to you in your ear" we were told. So, I was ready to go, after going through the moves with my tandem instructor. He was well over six foot tall and must have weighed about 16-17 stone. I am under five foot tall and about 10 stone. He was a very charming fellow and photos of us walking to the take off area show what a contrast in height we had. I was clipped on to my tandem when we sat on the floor of the little plane taking us up to jump out into the sunshine. It was so exciting to be eased forward to the open door of the plane, to be tipped out into the sky to freefall until after a few minutes our parachute was released, when we rose up before slowly descending earthwards. My tandem I think was amused by my height and age, and I think he decided to show off a bit. "Shall we do a twirl?" he asked. "Please yourself" I replied, knowing I had no control whatsoever on what was coming. The twirl meant that I was tipped headfirst toward the ground and spun round. I didn't like it much but made no comment. A little later, having had time to see the Solent, Isle of Wight, New Forest and away to the left Southampton, and to my right Dorset, he said, "Shall we twirl again?" "You're the driver," I replied.

I did not think of this at the time but had plenty of time to do so later. I think he had not paid enough attention first, to his altimeter, and secondly to the need for instruction into my ear. I had my knees bent up, as instructed in the gym, but he never gave the extend legs order, which is the position for landing. We hit the ground with my knees bent up. There was a gunshot in my ears as I fell forward, and I knew at once that I had dislocated my left ankle, and, probably I thought, fractured my tibia and fibula. Much of this caused by my large tandem chap falling, still attached, on top of me.

Gradually the pain intensified. I felt calm and in control whilst around me was much anxious activity. My instructor tandem apparently worked as a paramedic and when he offered the opinion that it would take at least two hours to get an ambulance to the airfield, I opted to take Jill's offer to take me by car to Odstock Hospital, Salisbury.

A painful journey followed in the back of the car, with my left ankle flapping in its very precarious situation as I watched my lower leg beginning to swell.

So began sixteen days in hospital, starting in A&E with indecision as to how the injury should be managed. I saw no senior staff from the orthopaedic department that day. I arrived at about 4.00 p.m. on a Saturday and with little analgesia attempts were made to stabilise a very unstable ankle joint. By 7.00 p.m. I was given ketamine whilst someone tried to manipulate the joint, only to make it even more unstable. This manoeuvre was the worst episode for me. Ketamine made me hallucinate in a terrifying way.

All this time Jill had stayed with me. We played "I went to Salisbury Hospital with… a hairdryer, cucumber, a picture of Cliff Richard, a diamond, a sausage roll etc" I felt humour was needed at this time, to keep up morâle and pass the time. Dear Jill eventually left me in A&E at 9.30 p.m. I was told I would go to theatre at 11.00 p.m., but at 2.00 a.m. I was found a bed instead in a small general surgical ward, Amesbury.

Next day I saw an orthopaedic surgeon and was able to see my x-rays, which showed a serious situation. I had torn the ends of the major ankle bone, the talus and also fractured both leg bones. These fractures also were in a spiral form and so difficult to stabilise. For ten days I endured external fixation of the limb whilst the surgeon waited for the swelling to subside enough to operate.

Thirteen silver screws and two silver plates were used to hold the left ankle and leg together. Mobilisation began and eventually I was able to return home with a clumsy boot, which fortunately protected my foot. I was free of this contraption by Christmas, and thanks to the fact that I have a stairlift, I was once more independent and able to be alone at home. Help from kind neighbours made it possible for me to gradually mobilise and get back to comparatively normal life again.

Hot on the trail of my recovery, enough to walk with a stick round the village, came the pandemic Covid-19. Since I was mostly confined to home anyway, the necessity for us to isolate did not affect me greatly. Neighbours and Jenny helped with shopping and other errands, and I stayed at home, tending my flower garden and vegetable patch. As summer progressed, I enjoyed meeting friends in my garden for drinks and meals, whilst obeying our government's instructions to keep the virus at bay, whilst work progressed to develop a vaccine. Although somewhat lame, I was happy to have raised £4,000 for Oakhaven. This was my swansong of efforts for the hospice, although I continue to give to my Extra Mile Award as I had, anonymously done each April for over 15 years. I was given descriptions in the Spring each year of what staff might have done over and above what their role in the day-to-day work in the hospice demanded of them. On that description, name unknown, I would select my Extra Mile winner. No names were ever mentioned, and the person receiving the extra pay on their month's payslip was directed not to speak of it. Thus, no-one could work for the award and no element of competition came about. The recipient must be involved with patient care to be eligible to be considered.

Latterly the new chairman of the Trust, naturally unaware of my award, started giving accolades with a public ceremony, but I still like the idea of an anonymous extra mile gift.

Whilst the service recognised by patients and their families remains the same as when I started the hospice, much has changed otherwise. With the expansion of the building itself so too there has been an increase in personnel, and with the bureaucracy inevitably accompanying it. All this increases the cost of running the hospice. I sometimes felt that there was a creation of jobs, all salaried, which perhaps could have been done voluntarily, so cutting cost.

The very distinctive logo, selected in 1988 by Phoebe, with its personal association with the Coates family has been discarded. Sadly the logo created in its place, to modernise the brand as explained to me, I find distressingly naïve. In design and colour, it is no longer eye catching, being one anaemic pseudo-oakleaf. I so wish the powers that be could have waited until, like Phoebe, I had died before changing this symbol of Oakhaven's origin.

I did not realise until I saw the new logo in place how upsetting I would find the change. I suppose it related to my loyalty to Phoebe and to our experiences together in those early days. It all seemed to have been given to us and part of the purpose to which we had committed ourselves. It is hard for me, in my late eighties to accept the eradication of something which meant so much to me.

I must concentrate now on the positive aspects of the time allotted to me. I still have so many blessings associated with my work. So many friendships and times of fun and laughter to look back on.

I write in a time of isolation in early 2021. When the covid 19 virus struck the country in 2020 so much changed. Not only domestically but nationally. The rate of increase in the death rate in those early months alarmed the country. Spread from the far east to the continent of Europe was uppermost in the news. It also coincided with Brexit and our much discussed final plans to leave the EU and go it alone. I had voted to stay in Europe. Many older people I think remembering the war years felt it was better to be together within the tent than to be outside it. The Trump years in America gave little comfort or confidence that they would be reliable allies. There was a vague feeling in some quarters that our decision would help to solve our immigration problems. I doubted that then and continue to do so now, as inflatable boats risk lives as desperate people take their chance to reach our shores across the hazardous waters of the English Channel.

Random Thoughts As Time Passes

Having written about my life from the 1930s until the 2020s it seems like a new narrative to ponder on present day living.

For me it is almost like a series of full stops with little content to the sentences in between. So many words emerging in the past year are new to me. Furlough, pandemic, distancing, bubbles and lockdown. Now all taken for granted. The development of a vaccine against this evil virus has given an element of hope of normality to come, but in March 2021 it seemed some way off. My days of swimming two or three times a week had long gone as only outdoor swimming was permitted. Visits from family, even a family wedding last year all became pipe dreams. So many people have had a far more distressing time. My only sadness has been loneliness. I would have experienced this I know even without the outbreak of a pandemic. As time has gone on the enthusiasm to make the best of a bad job has waned. After a dreary wet 20-21 winter, everyone became weary. Trying to be positive with so many restrictions given from government instruction has become trying, especially when they are given at last minute or changed so soon after one had got used to a new way of coping.

My plans for my beloved Alonnisos visits vary from one edict from on high to the next. I did visit in September 2020 but with a ticket booked for late May 2021, I fear that I shall have the summer at home.

Some positive things have come out of the shutdown. Whilst I am not an enthusiast for my laptop, I have managed to master Zoom. This has enabled me to join in conversations with committee members of our village community shop, which is to move to new premises when built, by the village hall. I even spoke to family, on their invitation. I would like to do it again. I have a weekly phone call from the family of my niece and nephew. Jenny calls most days, and we have met up, keeping our distance mostly outside.

Over the past three years I have joined the members of St John the Baptist Church, Boldre in their Lent Group. This year we have been paired with one another over the phone to discuss a poem each week in Lent. It is arranged by our Priest in Residence, Andrew Neaum. He has had an interesting career in many parts of the world. He was an Archdeacon in Australia. It was there he married his second wife Diana, who is a great asset to the community. Both had the experience of caring for their first partner until death.

Studying the poems selected by Andrew has taken me back to my childhood when Daddy read poetry to me, saying "Here's one you'll like". And, of course, I did.

When I was an active member of the Quakers, I enjoyed learning about the ethos of Friends and the history of the Society. I carry much of that with me still and in many ways it directs my way of life. I fail in many aspects I know, but their maxim that there is that of God in everyone gives a valuable pointer to live by. During the two years in which I studied for my MA Death and Society, I looked into the Quaker writings on many occasions.

Recently I found some notes I wrote at the time on spirituality. Another difficult topic which one has more time and inclination to ponder upon in later life. What do I mean by my Spiritual Journey? I wrote that it means different things to each of us. To me it describes the episodes in my life which have stayed with me and influenced me to realise we do not have all the answers and that there is another authority shaping and directing life. I have observed that let it alone can solve problems. Why? Is it divine intervention?

In my studies I read 'in the last analysis it is the concept of death which decides the answers to all the questions that life puts to us' (Douglas Davies 1960). This I understand. I also agreed with the writer Bethan Jones who wrote that beliefs are not static but are constantly revisioned depending on the individual's situation. I believe life experiences develop our spiritual understanding. Relationships and episodes in our lives move us on. So our beliefs change with time if we allow them too.

As I travel towards my 87th birthday, I take stock of the numerous experiences I have encountered over the years. I know I shall find so many memories popping up which I have not recorded as Father Time takes his toll and the odd remark or conversation with friends sets me conjuring up episodes in my past I have overlooked.

But it is time to close the book, before memory begins to play tricks.

I end recalling a life of great variety and contrasts. And

now? Simply the time to look back with gratitude and to look forward with hope.

2021

And Finally

As I write the last chapter of my story, I am joyful to say that I did get to Alonnisos in 2021. Despite the extra cost and complications from expensive tests to prove fitness to travel, I joined my niece Sarah and her husband Patrick flying to Thessaloniki and driving through mainland Greece to catch a ferry at Volos to Alonnisos. It was worth it to spend the month of June in the idyllic bay on the island containing Spiti Federico. Unfortunately two friends had flights cancelled, which meant I had three weeks alone in the deserted bay. However it was a perfect place to find peace and a time for total relaxation. My dear friends the Popkens were on the island and I was able to spend time with them and others. Especially with Julia Browne, the local agent for Greek Island Club. When I learned that my return flight had been cancelled I was at a loss as to how I would get home. Then one of my most exciting surprises came my way. When Friedrich learned of my dilemma, he called to say, "My son-in-law is flying to Skiathos on June 30 and you can fly home to Southampton in the plane!" I asked him to repeat what he had said. What a kind man. I can never thank him enough. I came home to be isolated for ten days, but the happiness of the holiday and flight home made it all worthwhile.

Even in old age exciting and unusual things are still happening.

Just landing at Southampton June 30th, 2021

Every year I wonder if it is my last time to see Alonnisos. I do hope I shall be there again.

But for now…

…It's where YOU finish!

- Pilley October 2021 -

Acknowledgements

When I was at sea, I met Ernest Hecht, of Souvenir Press. We were introduced by author Arthur Hayley who had been a pupil of my father, who he always acknowledged in the foreword to his books. Ernest was keen for me to write of my exploits at sea and wrote to me several times asking how the book was coming along. It wasn't.

Fifty years later I have at last recorded so much more than my nautical years. Writing a memoir is a challenging experience but so worthwhile.

I could not have made progress without the loyal support of my Oakhaven secretary, Judy Hallett, who came out of retirement to make my efforts fit for publication. I cannot thank Judy and her husband George enough for their patience and practical help.

My daughter Jenny Rimbault more than made up for my computer ignorance and her professional skills and advice have been greatly valued.

In the course of my writing I have met more talented people willing to advise and progress my effort. Photographer Luke Parkinson and artist Anna Sims have been generous with their time and expertise in producing artwork both for the cover and illustrations. Serenedipity led me to Carlsen's Antiques and Fine Art gallery where dear owner Dimitri located Anna for me. Thank you.

Finally I know it would be difficult to find a more supportive publisher than Keith Abbott of Michael Terence Publishing. A constant and patient source of help.

Many thanks to them all.

I hope anyone who finds themselves mentioned in the text will be forgiving of any lapses in memory on my part and will not find anything contentious in my narrative.

It is my intention to use the book as a fund-raiser for my hospice, Oakhaven at Lymington, Hampshire. I hope my efforts may prove fruitful to a charity so dear to me.

- Jan Swallow October 2021

Available worldwide from Amazon

Michael Terence Publishing

www.mtp.agency

www.facebook.com/mtp.agency

@mtp_agency